ENGLISH IN GLOBAL CONTEXTS

PROFICIENCY TASKS FOR ASPIRING LEARNERS

JJ POLK

GLOBAL TOUCHSTONES

English in Global Contexts:
Proficiency Tasks for Aspiring Learners

ISBN: 978-0-9909086-2-3

Published by:
Global Touchstones
Los Angeles, CA

Cover and interior design by Stacey Aaronson

Printed in the United States of America

CONTENTS

PREFACE

Whether as native speakers or as second-language learners, students of English who wish to excel in their communication skills must acquire both an extensive, active vocabulary and keen insight into the appropriate contexts in which the words they learn are used. For advanced students, the acquisition of higher-level lexis also requires mastery of often perplexing syntactic patterns that may vary significantly across genres. *English in Global Contexts* has been designed with the advanced learner in mind. All the tasks and activities contained in this volume are topic-based and can be completed in either a classroom environment or (with limitations) a self-study regimen.

Each unit opens with a topic-based reading passage with either an embedded cloze task or a word form-related activity. (Both types of tasks have traditionally been a component of Cambridge ESOL examinations.) Follow-up vocabulary tasks enable students to attain a greater appreciation for the richness of the English language, while recycling phrases and synonyms of key lexical elements from the text. Language focus questions and an accompanying explanatory Appendix highlight important lexico-grammatical structures in the authentic context of the content-related reading tasks.

All units contain a cryptic "Ultimate Challenge," which requires the learner to reconstruct a sentence in which all the words have been jumbled. We suggest this activity be completed in teams as a competitive language game. Since all the deconstructed sentences are true statements that can be inferred from the opening text passage, the activity also hones the student's reading comprehension skills. Dedicated self-study students who enjoy cryptograms or crossword puzzles will also find the "Ultimate Challenge" to be an enjoyable and instructive pastime.

Students who bring with them an innate curiosity about the world will find the follow-up discussion and debate topics stimulating. Questions in these sections target the production of natural discourse on topics of global interest. Programs geared toward the undergraduate population / university preparation and exam classes will benefit from the focused research writing topics suggested at the end of each unit.

J J Polk
November, 2014

UNIT 1

HE SAYS ... SHE SAYS

BEFORE YOU READ

What expectations exist in your culture of the way men and women are supposed to behave? What are some examples of "typical boy" / "typical girl" things to do?

CLOZE TASK

DIRECTIONS: As you read the following text, fill in the numbered blanks with ONE suitable word.

A Besides the blatant anatomical differences that [1]______________ men from women, there are also less obvious features attributed to the mind itself that set men and women [2]______________________. One common complaint heard from many women around the world concerns the seemingly ubiquitous male ability to sit glued in [3]_______________ of a TV or computer screen when certain sports events are broadcast. Singularly transfixed on the play-by-play development of the game, these men seem thoroughly capable of tuning [4]______________________ any and all other human or natural occurrences that might attempt to compete with the sporting event for air time—earthquakes, tornadoes, fires, robberies at gunpoint. It's anyone's [5]______________________ how many wives around the world have successfully taken advantage of the situation by saying: "Honey, I just wanted to let you know that your sister and I are going shopping at the mall, and we're going to use your credit card since ours are maxed out. You don't mind, do you?"—knowing full well what the answer will be: "Yeah, sure, see you later! Man, did you see that pass?"

B And this brings us to that one common habit perennially ranked near the top of nearly every male's list of pet peeves: the quite uncanny female capacity to shop until she drops, particularly at clothing sales.

C With many shopping malls around the world now encompassing a hundred or more retail stores—a full half of which might be devoted [6]_______ the seemingly endless varieties of women's clothes—the unlucky husband who happens to find [7]________________ on a shopping outing with his wife, her friends, or her sisters must arm himself mentally with all [8]____________________ science has to offer. Male victims of the female shopping spree must frequently be carried out on stretchers that stand ready at the waiting for just such occasions.

Image production credit: iStock.com/Maica

D The prototypical female shopping enthusiast [9]________________ a store, approaches the first rack of clothes that looks promising, and begins a ritual that strikes fear into the heart of virtually every male on the planet. The first item is [10]___________ from the rack and held up for comment by all accompanying members of the coterie. It is first turned clockwise, then counter-clockwise. Next it is turned upside-down and inside-out, held up against similar items for inspection, caressed, smoothed out, and perhaps even smelled. "Oh, I love the color, but I [11]________________ how well it will go with the shoes I bought this morning. Do you think they might have it in a lighter shade of teal? Should I ask them if they have it in ecru?"

E But of course that's only the first item. And, that's only the first rack. There are 142 other items on this rack; there are also 55 other racks to look through, with the same expanded rituals potentially replicated with every item of interest. And that's only the first floor. There are three additional floors, [12]____________________ with just as many racks, all with tempting blouses, pants, bras, business suits, travel suits, lingerie, party wear, formalwear, beachwear, picnic wear, and sports outfits—all in a never-ending chromatic palette of chartreuse, hot pink, android green, baby blue, beau blue, bondi blue, bisque, bistre, blanched almond, boysenberry, burnt orange, cinnamon, champagne, cobalt, copper, coral red, cornell red, dark candy apple red, carnation red, and thousands more shades of violet, beige, blue, brown, green, and yellow. [13]__________ mind that the average male brain cannot even tell the difference between turquoise and teal (and likely doesn't care one way or the other), much [14]____________________ remember their impossible names.

F The anxious tag-along senses a glimmer of hope and relief [15]____________________ after the three-and-a-half-hour tour, all are assembled near the exit door. Alas, even the humblest expectations come to nought with the realization that that was only the first store! There are 47 others, each with just as many floors and racks and blouses and pants, and shoes and belts and bras in every conceivable texture, shape, and designer name. All of which need to be held out for inspection and comment, and perhaps even [16]______________ on in the fitting room with a full-length [17]___________ providing the ultimate test of feminine approval.

G But this is not to [18]______________ that the male of our species is immune to shopping enthusiasm himself—[19]___________ from it. Just look at what happens to the male brain in the computer game showroom. Many men are capable of spending hours with hands and fingers glued to the joystick of the latest model of gaming computer, with the hypnotically monotonous tones of technical wizardry filling in beautifully for superfluous conversation. And when an enthusiast [20]__________________ upon someone who shares his zeal for the same model, instant bonding seems to occur, with outings to upcoming gamer conferences planned on the fly. No communication in verbal terms seems necessary for the tech titans to feel as if they've known each other for years, and in the [21]____________________ that actual sentence-based exchanges do occur, the incomprehensibly rambling gibberish, devoid of any recognizable form of syntax, can even effect an entire series of insider giggles. For many master gamers, the hours spent in communion locked to their favorite joystick are the closest thing to earthly heaven.

Image production credit: iStock.com/meshapho

H These observed gender-specific behavior patterns may differ greatly from culture to culture and most certainly from individual to individual. As such, they are mere starting points, generalizations as opposed to stereotypes. There are, [22]____________________ all, many women who abhor shopping, just as there are men who [23]____________________ sportscasts on television.

I But one thing is for certain: advertisers thrive on the use of stereotypical gender roles in targeting specific groups of customers through marketing campaigns. The soft, delicate silhouette of a beautiful woman nicely complements the latest fragrances from the perfume houses of Paris; the rough, sweaty footballer segues nicely into the after-game brand-name beer. Reversing the images readily reveals perhaps just how brainwashed we have all become.

J In the sober world of science, gender [24]____________________ reflected in stereotypical behavior patterns remain a puzzle. Many researchers would cite "hard-wiring" schemas within the respective neural networks themselves as the primary source of such traits. Early gender-based studies involving task-based performances appeared to confirm that significant regions on both sides of the female brain seemed to be much better at linking or communicating with one another. This might [25]_________________ how many housewives seem to have no problem at all with cooking a full five-course meal, ironing [26]_______________, changing a baby's diaper, holding an engaging telephone [27]__________, and paying bills online, all at the same time! Evolutionary biologists see these feats as part and parcel of our own primate heritage as hunter-gatherers. While the men of the tribes were hunting in expeditions in focused pursuit of promising prey, the women would remain at home tending to the care and education of the children. The women needed to remain highly alert for marauding predators and other types of dangers that presented themselves in the wild. The women could thus [28]________________________ the children and tend to all the chores while listening intently for the arrival of potential danger. The female's attention has always been omni-directional, [29]________________________ in a multitude of impressions, but simultaneously focused. And what is more, the "female touch" mediated much-needed compassion and concern for the well-being of others (Myers, 2008). Today, we know that the maternal display of tender loving care ("TLC") is somehow crucial to epigenetic changes that are still not understood.

K A number of early studies conducted using functional magnetic resonance imaging (fMRI) appeared to point to a greater degree of lateralization—or hemispheric dominance—in the brains of men and to more bilateral neural activity in women, particularly when subjects were asked to perform language-related tasks (Phillips, Lowe, Lurito, Dzemidzic & Mathews, 2001). But recently, both the experimental design and underlying assumptions of a [30]_____________________ of such studies have been reexamined in a more critical light (Sommer, Aleman, Bouma & Kahn, 2004). The seemingly "natural" dichotomization of gender roles and behavior patterns led rather seamlessly to the expectation that major gender-based differences would also be discovered in the actual physical brains of men and women. As cogently argued by Kaiser, Haller, Schmitz & Nitsch (2009), the expectation of such dissimilarities (as opposed to similarities) "has continued to dominate neuroscientific concepts." In fact, studies that demonstrate such differences have enjoyed a much greater probability of [31]______________________ published than those highlighting traits that are shared between [32]______________________.

L Even more important, a wide range of research has begun to emphasize the enormous plasticity of our biological brains. [33]____________ from being mechanistic, hard-wired, chip-like entities that mindlessly dictate terms of behavior, the very molecular components of our brains ("nature") respond to environmental stimuli ("nurture") and adapt accordingly. [34]______________ has been shown particularly in studies involving individuals who have undergone extensive musical training (Münte, Altenmüller & Jäncke, 2002; Schlaug, Jäncke, Huang, Staiger & Steinmetz, 1995) as well as in many of the miraculous recovery efforts of stroke victims.

M The current paradigm in behavior research points to a highly dynamic relationship between nature and nurture. Without our physical brains and the inherent abilities they [35]______________________ us with, we would have no experience in the material world at all. But who we are and what we ultimately become in life greatly depend on the loving care our parents provide us and on the wealth of experiences, both positive and negative, that we encounter in life.

N Nevertheless, it may be difficult for all of us to transcend the genetic blueprint that nature has engrained in us. In 2014, a team of psychologists and primatologists reported the remarkable results of a longitudinal study they had conducted on young chimpanzees at Gombe National Park in Tanzania (von Lonsdorf et al., 2014). The chief aim of the 34-year study was to investigate "the evolutionary and biological bases of sex differences in behaviour" among our closest relatives. The study observed striking differences in the behavior patterns of the young chimps, even at a very early age, strongly suggesting that the gender differences are indeed innate.

REFERENCES

Kaiser, A., Haller, S., Schmitz, S. & Nitsch, C. (2009). On sex/gender-related similarities and differences in fMRI language research. *Brain Research Reviews*, *61*(2), 49–59.

von Lonsdorf, E., Anderson, K., Stanton, M., Shender, M., Heintz, M., Goodall, J. & Murray, C. M. (2014). Boys will be boys: Sex differences in wild infant chimpanzee social interactions. *Animal Behavior*, *88*, 79–83.

Münte, T., Altenmüller, E. & Jäncke, L. (2002). The musician's brain as a model of neuroplasticity. Nature Reviews, *Neuroscience*, *3*(6), 473–478.

Myers, S. (2008). *On being a woman: Musings of a radical mother.* Bloomington, IN: Trafford Publishing.

Phillips, M., Lowe, M., Lurito, J., Dzemidzic, M. & Mathews, V. (2001). Temporal lobe activation demonstrates sex-based differences during passive listening. *Radiology*, *220*(1), 202–207.

Schlaug, G., Jäncke, L., Huang, Y., Staiger, J. & Steinmetz, H. (1995). Increased corpus callosum size in musicians. *Neuropsychologia*, *33*(8), 1047–1055.

Sommer, I., Aleman, A., Bouma, A. & Kahn, R. (2004). Do women really have more bilateral language representation than men? A meta-analysis of functional imaging studies. *Brain*, *127*(8), 1845–1852.

POST-READING QUESTIONS

1. In what ways do you personally "fit in" with any of the gender-specific behaviors described in the text?
2. What citation format is used in the text?
3. The text could probably be divided into at least two genres according to the audience / purpose of the text and the language used.
   A) Where does the more serious, academic style of writing begin?
   B) What are some examples of the tongue-in-cheek humor used in the first part?
4. How did your view of gender-specific behavior change after reading this article?
5. What does the author mean with the phrase "just how brainwashed we have all become" at the end of paragraph I?
6. In your own words, summarize evolutionary biologists' views on the inherent nature of gender-specific behavior patterns.
7. Describe the meaning of "plasticity" as the term is used in relation to neurological / cognitive processes.

8. In your own words, paraphrase the arguments presented on both sides of the nature *versus* nurture divide with respect to gender-specific behavior.

VOCABULARY WORK

PART A

From the reading text, find the words or phrases that have similar meanings to the words / phrases given in the numbered lists below. The first one has been done for you as an example.

From Paragraphs A–G:	Synonymous Word or Phrase
1. fondled; touched gently	caressed (paragraph D)
2. continually; perpetually; recurringly	________________
3. most modest; most unpretentious	________________
4. the art and skill of a magician or warlock	________________
5. incredible; unbelievable; astounding; strange; weird	________________
6. pertaining to colors	________________
7. ascribed to; assigned to; credited with	________________
8. unnecessary; unneeded; not required	________________
9. outing; fling; adventure; romp	________________
10. overt; obvious	________________
11. on pins and needles; restless; antsy; apprehensive	________________
12. lacking; deprived of; wanting; without	________________
13. everywhere	________________
14. grain; structure; fabric; surface	________________
15. cots (especially for medical use); pallets	________________
16. verbal nonsense; jabber	________________
17. wandering; unfocused; uneven; erratic	________________
18. aired (verb); televised	________________
19. enticing; alluring	________________

20. nothing; nil ____________
21. related to the structure of the body ____________
22. unvarying; unchanging; dull; boring ____________
23. adventures; pleasure trips; excursions ____________
24. repeated; reproduced; reduplicated ____________

From Paragraphs H–N: Synonymous Word or Phrase

25. deeds; achievements ____________
26. outline; contour; profile; shape ____________
27. emphasizing; pointing out; stressing ____________
28. chase; hunt; quest ____________
29. to transition uninterruptedly from one point or element to another ____________
30. effectively; pertinently; forcefully; persuasively; authoritatively; convincingly ____________
31. scents; aromas ____________
32. elements; parts ____________
33. pliability; malleability; flexibility; adaptability ____________
34. riddle; mystery; enigma ____________
35. empathy; mercy; sympathy; pity; kind-heartedness ____________
36. to quote; to refer to ____________

VOCABULARY WORK

PART B

Choose an appropriate form of one of the words given below to complete the numbered sentences that follow. Two of the words have been used twice.

ATTRIBUTE	MONOTONY
BLATANT	PURSUIT
BROADCAST	RAMBLE
COGENT	REPLICATION
COMPONENT	SEGUE
FEAT	SUPERFLUOUS
HIGHLIGHT	UBIQUITOUS

1. In many cities, significant increases in air pollution have rightly been ____________________ to a substantial rise in the numbers of private cars.

2. Most of our editing work on the manuscript involved eliminating redundancies and other _________________________ verbiage.

3. In the Constitution of the United States of America, "life, liberty, and the _________________________ of happiness" are declared to be inalienable rights granted to all human beings.

4. The results of studies purportedly showing neutrinos traveling faster than the speed of light could not be _________________________, thus casting doubt on the methods of measurement used in the experiments.

5. Declining reading, math, and science test scores in many western countries have _________________________ the need for fresh approaches to teaching and curriculum design.

6. Throughout much of the industrial era, major manufacturers showed a _________________________ disregard for the environment by dumping thousands of tons of toxic waste into rivers, streams, and oceans.

7. With its 787 carbon fiber composite aircraft, Boeing embarked on a questionable approach to manufacturing the jet, as essentially all of its _________________________ parts are constructed separately in many different countries and are then flown back to the U.S. for final assembly.

8. When ________________________ dangerous criminals, Interpol makes extensive use of continent-wide databases containing millions of images that are quickly processed using highly accurate face recognition software.

9. In regions of the world that do not experience four distinct seasons, periodic changes often ________________________ so smoothly and subtly from one into the other that many observers might find it difficult to describe what changes were even noticeable.

10. Neutrinos are among nature's most ________________________ particles, with as many as 65 billion per second passing through every square centimeter of any region on earth perpendicular to the sun, including our own bodies.

11. Most of the students in the lecture were put to sleep by the speaker's unwavering, ________________________ voice.

12. One of the worst things any candidate for a job opening can do during an interview is to ________________________ aimlessly from topic to topic without any clear focus.

13. Every four years, most people around the world are able to view live ________________________ of the opening ceremonies of the Olympics.

14. Johann Sebastian Bach's extemporaneous composition and performance of a four-part fugue was described by MIT artificial intelligence expert Douglas Hofstatter as a super-human ________________________, equivalent to playing 64 games of chess blindfolded and winning all of them.

15. In the wake of the 2008 global financial crisis, international teams of legal and economic experts ________________________ argued the case for an international regulatory body to supervise complex markets such as those involving derivatives.

16. Many high-tech industries rely on rare earth elements for a number of ________________________ in their most advanced products.

LANGUAGE FOCUS

PART C

1. In paragraphs A–H, identify 10 unreduced relative clauses and specify the noun or pronoun that they modify. [For a review of the grammar of RELATIVE CLAUSES, see the APPENDIX, section B.]

2. In paragraphs A–H, identify four reduced relative clauses and specify the noun or pronoun that they modify.

3. Identify one reduced relative clause that has been placed at the beginning of the sentence, pre-positional to the noun subject it modifies.

4. Identify words or phrases of middle to low register that indicate familiarity or emotional closeness. [For a review of REGISTER in English, see the APPENDIX, section A.]

5. What does the pronoun "others" refer to in the phrase in paragraph F: "There are 47 others …"?

Sentence Transformation

For questions 6–10, use the word given below the first sentence to complete the second sentence in the blanks provided. Use between three and eight words including the given word. The given word must NOT be changed in any way, and the meaning of the sentences should be as similar as possible.

Example: We eagerly await a renewed encounter with you in the future.
forward
We are really looking forward to seeing you again in the future.

6. No one knows the number of people who suffer from some form of addiction.
   guess
   It's ______________________________ people suffer from some form of addiction.

7. Carlos can't even balance his own checkbook, let alone someone else's.
   mention
   Carlos can't even balance his own checkbook, ________________ someone else's.

8. It's often difficult to distinguish identical twins if you look solely at physical features.

   tell

   It's often difficult ________________________ if you look solely at physical features.

9. Your son is quite lazy, but he can still pass the course if he tries his best.

   say

   Your son is quite lazy, but that is ________________________ the course if he tries his best.

10. The mediation board will resolve any disputes that might arise in the future.

    ironed

    Future disputes will ________________________ the mediation board.

PART D

Sentence Reconstruction

ULTIMATE CHALLENGE

Reconstruct the following ten sentences by putting the individual words back into their correct order. All of the sentences represent TRUE statements that can be inferred from the information presented in the reading text ("He Says ... She Says") at the beginning of this unit. Add any necessary punctuation.

1. of from the and combined behavior specific effects result gender most nature patterns nurture likely

   ____

   ____

   ____

2. in the that to from early argue role female her multitask human superior evolutionary ability care biologists societies derives giving

   ____

   ____

   ____

3. the to them around during oblivious fans enthusiastic world events appear often male sporting

4. to of the the and are between female attempting inconclusive brain clear findings prove studies male distinctions

5. do to to men women attention seem colors than more pay

6. their to do want thoughts male always game verbalize not enthusiasts

7. to on their routinely roles advertisers gender rely market stereotypical products

8. the is as and than that have immutable recent brain believed shown previously plastic studies and dynamic static rather

9. the on that that than those do of a studies genders differences similarities getting gender between published enjoy focus emphasize likelihood greater

____

____

____

10. the to that the the on of from early cognitive investigating training adapts musical environment brain effects input actively development studies confirm

____

____

____

PART E

LANGUAGE IN USE

I Suggested Questions for Discussion

A. Present cogent arguments for either of the following positions:

i) Gender-specific behavior patterns are inherent traits reflecting our genetic makeup and can thus not be altered.

ii) Though biologically based, gender-specific behavior patterns are largely the result of education and socialization and are thus highly malleable.

B. Is it possible that there are as many "genders" in human behavior as there are people on the planet? Give reasons to support your view.

C. Should young children be trained and educated to conform to socially accepted, gender-specific behavior patterns? Weigh the advantages and disadvantages of both sides of this issue.

II Suggested Questions for Written Research Projects

A. If gender-specific behavior patterns are largely biologically determined, why have gender roles and gender role models changed or shifted so dramatically over the centuries?

B. If gender-specific behavior and roles are largely based in human biology, what are the arguments in favor of treating humans equally with the same opportunities provided to all, irrespective of these differences?

C. Describe and outline your own topic-related research question.

IT TAKES ALL KINDS OF PEOPLE

UNIT 2

BEFORE YOU READ

Describe a person who you feel is very similar to you. Describe a person who seems to be your exact opposite. What are the special characteristics of these two people?

DIRECTIONS: As you read the following text, complete the blanks after the numbered brackets with an appropriate form of the word given in capital letters. The first one has been done for you as an example.

CLOZE TASK

A Common sense should tell us that there are probably as many types of people in the world as there are humans on the planet, each with his or her own individual [0] PERSON personality. But is this really the case?

B In 1921, Swiss [1] PSYCHE________________ Carl Gustav Jung published a theory of "psychological types," which became the basis for further refinement and development by other subsequent profilers of the human psyche. Katherine Briggs and her daughter Isabel Briggs Myers expanded on the framework laid out by Jung in their renowned type indicator. With between two and three million assessments given per year, the Myers-Briggs Type Indicator (MBTI) is one of the most commonly used personality evaluation tools found anywhere in the world. Despite various forms of [2] CRITIC________________ (Michael, 2003) that have been leveled against the personality typing apparatus, corporations and other organizations continue to rely on input from the MBTI results. In fact, in at least one study of corporate performance, an entire company was identified by its "characteristic" four-letter Myers-Briggs Type Indicator [3] DESIGNATE________________ (Garrety, 2007). (Those who are interested in [4] DETERMINE________________ their four-letter type can use any number of Internet sites featuring a battery of questions. These websites allow users to click through possible responses designed to assess the individual's personality. Many provide an "answer key" with a [5] DESCRIBE________________ evaluation of the given profile, including information on ideal career choices as well as characteristic strengths and [6] WEAK________________.)

C Myers-Briggs and its original Jungian framework (Jung, 1921/1971) dichotomize human personalities according to four pairs of fundamental traits or features. The first of these dichotomies—that of extroverts and introverts—is based on the simple inward versus outward [7] DIRECT ________________ of a person's thoughts and feelings. Extroverts are classified as people who are outwardly [8] DIRECT______________, i.e., individuals who derive their energy and [9] JOY______________ from encounters with people and situations external to the self. Extroverts seek out the company of others and feel at their best in groups of friends and [10] ACQUAINT____________________. Introverts, in contrast, tend to occupy their minds with inner reflection centered on ideas and [11] SPECULATE______________ about possibilities, values, choices, and outcomes. If forced to stay at home alone [12] PONDER______________ the significance of some abstruse philosophical concept, the "typical" extrovert would likely quickly become restless, bored, and lonely, whereas the large social [13] GATHER______________ with dozens of strangers, all [14] ENERGY_________ and engaged in [15] OBLIGE____________ small talk, might have the "typical" introvert looking for the nearest exit. Feeling exhausted from the extended interaction with others, the introvert will probably want to spend the next five days in quiet isolation, slowly recuperating from the unwanted social outing.

D These two fundamental attitudes are further complemented in the personality profiling schema by dichotomous functions: feeling / thinking;

sensing / intuiting; and judging / perceiving. In combination, the four sets of pairs yield a total of 16 distinct personality types, each with special talents and tendencies. Professional headhunters and [16] RECRUIT__________ agencies often use the personality type profile in [17] COMBINE ________________ with a given job description to match hopeful [18] APPLY____________ with the skills required for and demands found in employment positions (Jessup, 2002).

E Of course it must be noted that the [19] BOUND____________ between many of the psychological types are often fairly fluid, with many individuals falling somewhere in the golden middle of any two extremes. At the same time, however, many experts in the field of profiling point out that we all have tendencies and [20] INCLINE________________ that dominate or win out over others, and that it is these [21] DOMINATE ______________ traits that are revealed in our exclusive four-letter type.

F Whether we fall into the category of "sensing" or "intuiting" depends on whether we choose to trust the information conveyed to us primarily through our eyes and ears, or whether we instead rely on our "gut feelings," a type of inner instinct that somehow "tells" us what the correct [22] CHOOSE ____________ of action or the right response to a given problem is. Likewise, do we allow our feelings (the "F" in the "F/T" dichotomy) for someone or for a situation to sway us toward a given course of action, as opposed to [23] ALLOW ____________ our "better [24] JUDGE____________" ("T") based on logic and facts to lead us? And lastly, do our innermost selves force us to summarily assess, order, and critique ("J" in the "J/P" dichotomy) the world around us, or are we rather content to simply take it all in ("P") and to allow the world to be as ambiguous as it wants, without our passing judgment on it?

G The most useful of the dichotomous pairs with respect to the people we encounter on a daily basis is surely the aforementioned introvert/ extrovert opposition. Like most authors before her, Susan Cain (2012) also describes the key difference between the two personality types in relation to the sort of environment a person prefers. Extroverts tend to go in for the louder, more [25] VIBRATE______________ party atmosphere in a room full of strangers, whereas introverts seek out the quietude of low-key, subdued surroundings with as little external stimulation as possible. The typical introvert would opt for an intimate conversation with a close friend any day over the boisterous, pulsating energy of a frat-house party.

H Cain also contends that the United States in particular went through a profound transformation at the turn of the twentieth century. Big Business itself was centered on the demands for the quick sales pitch and aggressive [26] MARKET______________ platforms, and what better way to fulfill those goals than to employ the hard-hitting, 300-word-per-minute extrovert who could talk his way into the hearts and minds of even the most reluctant customers! This trend served to promote a "culture of personality"—and the concomitant people-oriented, [27] CHARISMA ______________, extroverted "talker"—at the expense of the more [28] REFLECT______________ introverted thinker, whose values were more clearly at home in a "culture of character" as [29] BODY______________ in the person of Abraham Lincoln.

Image production credit: iStock.com/jhorrocks

I Today, there is a trend back toward the [30] APPRECIATE ______________________ of the introverted mindset. Despite the fact that today's workplaces have largely been designed with the extroverted employee in mind and tend to favor teamwork, as Cain has noted, recent studies conducted by Adam Grant (2013) at the University of Pennsylvania's Wharton School of Business have shown that the introverted leader tends to bring out the best in [31] CREATE______________ employees by giving the latter the freedom and space to develop their ideas. In contrast, the more extroverted leader tends to want to dominate the flow of ideas in accordance with his or her own [32] CONCEIVE______________ notions of what the final outcome should be. At the same time, [33] NUMBER __________ studies have shown quite [34] CONVINCE______________ that the hyper-competitive atmosphere [35] FURTHER______________ by the traditional push for the aggressive sales pitch has in many cases led to complete failure for a number of corporations. CEOs who alienate all those around them with their overly domineering and aggressive personalities have often witnessed their firms fall deeper and deeper in the red as leadership forsakes long-term planning and harmonious [36] LABOR ______________ (the "Toyota model") for the sake of short-term goals and spite-inspiring one-upmanship.

J Two "opposite" personality profiles from the spectrum of 16 illustrate just how truly different Myers-Briggs "types" are. ESTP personalities have been described as the life of the party. Suave, sophisticated, debonair, they exude charm and charisma. In the presence of ESTPs, there is never a dull moment. In the blink of an eye, their magnetic charm can catapult them into the limelight to lead a team of international [37] NEGOTIATE______________________ or into the position of leading diplomat of a country. Living forever in the here and now, they tend to favor a pragmatic approach to problem solving.

K At the other extreme is the prototypical solitary writer, the INFJ. These people have almost uncanny powers of intuition, sensing the innermost secrets of those around them and somehow, almost magically, comprehending the entire scope of human events on a grandiose philosophical scale. Statistically, INFJs constitute only 1% to 4% of the population, the rarest of the 16 types. Owing to their intensely creative inner life, they tend to be very private, aloof, and perhaps even difficult to get to know. Using their capacity for empathy, astute knack for languages, and active imagination, they can become very gifted novelists, psychologists, or philosophers who attempt to fathom the depths of existence, space, and time.

Image production credit: iStock.com/ajaelh

L Online dating services [38] REPORT___________ make extensive use of personality profiles by attempting to "match" candidates with the "best fit" for what experience has shown works best together and for what both people are looking for in a potential partner. Over time, many of us develop a fairly [39] RELY____________ feeling for what types of people we most easily harmonize with, and what types we should do our best to avoid. The question is, do those chosen soulmates—or conversely, nemeses—actually correspond to any reliable four-letter type?

M It should also be noted that "norms," even in their most individual forms of expression, are very strongly influenced by [40] CULTURE _____________ mediated behavior patterns. In some countries, singing and dancing in public appear to fit in quite well with standard expectations of public life. In cities such as Los Angeles, many drivers on the city's extensive system of freeways have been known to cruise down the highways singing out the windows and jiggling their bottoms in their seats, barely able to contain their enthusiasm for life or the music blaring from the radio. In more reserved countries like Finland, such exuberant public displays of enthusiasm might be seen as a clear indication that the individual was suffering from a psychotic episode.

N With the global expansion of vast sectors of manufacturing and [41] FINANCE______________ operations, corporate executives have become acutely aware of the importance of personality and intercultural interaction among employees and [42] MANAGE______________ alike (Bennet, Aston & Colguhoun, 2000; Caligiuri, 2000; Paul, 2000; Saner, Yiu & Sondergaard, 2000; Tung, 1993). At the same time, certain features of human harmony and discord know no boundaries across cultures. As in [43] MARRY_________________, some couples and teams, quite irrespective of their countries or cultures of origin, seem to [44] HARMONY________________ so naturally that it might appear they were simply destined for each other. At the opposite extreme are individuals who would never give each other the time of day, or who might lie [45] WAKE______________ at night seeding plans for revenge because of behavior patterns perceived and interpreted as [46] MALICE___________.

O By the very nature of their areas of [47] EXPERT______________, human resource [48] SPECIAL_________________ and family counselors [49] CONSIST______________ have their work cut out for them in their attempts to mediate between people who display seemingly [50] RECONCILE______________ differences. How we choose to express ourselves and to interpret the world of people and things around us is as much a part of our cultural surroundings as it is an expression of our individual wants and needs. Those who feel more at home combing the sands of a beach alone at sunset are no less "weird" than the shaking, rocking/rolling frat boy who has opted for the spontaneous rave in a crowd of 3,000. Who can say what factors of nature or nurture have combined to create the two extremes?

REFERENCES

Bennett, R., Aston, A. & Colguhoun, T. (2000). Cross-cultural training: A critical stage in ensuring the success of international assignments. *Human Resource Management Journal, 39*(2/3), 239–250.

Cain, S. (2012). *Quiet: The power of introverts in a world that can't stop talking.* New York: The Crown Publishing Group.

Caligiuri, P. (2000). Selecting expatriates for personality characteristics: A moderating effect on personality on the relationship between host national contact and cross-cultural adjustment. *Management International Review, 40*(1), 61–80.

Garrety, K. (2007). Beyond ISTJ: A discourse-analytic study of the use of the Myers-Briggs Type Indicator as an organisational change device in an Australian industrial firm. *Asia Pacific Journal of Human Resources, 45*(2), 218–234.

Grant, A. (2013). Rethinking the extraverted sales ideal: The ambivert advantage, *Psychological Science, 24*(6), 1024–1030.

Jessup, C. M. (2002). Applying psychological types and 'gifts differing' to organizational change. *Journal of Organizational Change Management, 15*(5), 502–511.

Jung, C. (1921/1971). *Psychological types: The collected works of C. G. Jung* (Vol. 6). Bollingen Series XX. Princeton, NJ: Princeton University Press.

Michael, J. (2003). Using the Myers-Briggs Type Indicator as a tool for leadership development? Apply with caution. *Journal of Leadership and Organizational Studies, 10*(1), 68–81.

Paul, H. (2000). Creating a global mindset. *Thunderbird International Business Review, 42*(2), 187–200.

Saner, R., Yiu, L. & Sondergaard, M. (2000). Business diplomacy management: A core competency for global companies. *Academy of Management Executive, 14*(1), 80–92.

Tung, R. (1993). Managing cross-national and intra-national diversity. *Human Resource Management, 32*(4), 461–477.

POST-READING QUESTIONS

1. While reading the text, did you feel you would more likely fall into the category of "introvert" or "extrovert"?
2. Are the differences or the similarities between people more important? Why?

3. Why might it be important to classify or to "type" people into different categories?
4. Can you think of other fundamental distinctions that might exist among humans?
5. How did your views of yourself and of your friends change after reading this article?
6. In your own words, describe the differences between extroverts and introverts.
7. Describe how the personalities of corporate CEOs can impact company performance.
8. In your own words, summarize the most salient information presented in this reading passage.

VOCABULARY WORK

PART A

From the reading text, find the words or phrases that have similar meanings to the words / phrases given in the numbered lists below. The first one has been done for you as an example.

From Paragraphs A–G:	Synonymous Word or Phrase
1. look for; try to find	seek out (paragraph C)
2. transmitted (as for example information)	____________
3. clamorous; rocking; noisy; rowdy	____________
4. aimed at; pointed at; brought against	____________
5. famous; well known	____________
6. satisfied; pleased; at ease	____________
7. played down; understated; toned down; subdued	____________
8. series; suite; set	____________
9. changing; flowing; shifting	____________
10. results; consequences	____________
11. recovering; getting better; on the mend	____________
12. extract; obtain; secure; get; procure	____________

13. quiet; hushed; tranquil; peaceful ____________
14. ensuing; following; succeeding; next ____________
15. emphasize; underscore; highlight; stress ____________
16. win over; talk into; influence; convince; bring around ____________
17. equivocal; ambivalent; indefinite; vague ____________
18. previously cited or referenced ____________

From Paragraphs H–O: Synonymous Word or Phrase

19. evoke; elicit; extract ____________
20. hesitant; disinclined; averse to; unwilling ____________
21. attendant; accompanying ____________
22. comprehend; understand; probe the depths of ____________
23. urbane; gracious; elegant; refined ____________
24. reserved; reticent; frosty; standoffish ____________
25. notoriety; eminence; fame; prominence ____________
26. dissonance; disharmony; conflict ____________
27. to be adapted to; to harmonize with ____________
28. exhilarated; ebullient; vivacious; profuse ____________
29. estrange; shut out; exclude ____________
30. launch; propel ____________
31. chose; selected ____________
32. mentally deranged; insane ____________
33. mortal enemies; foes ____________
34. wading through; sifting through; screening; sorting through ____________

35. a boisterous dance party ____________________

36. practical; utilitarian; businesslike ____________________

37. being in debt; operating at a loss ____________________

38. boring; unexciting; tiresome ____________________

PART B

VOCABULARY WORK

Choose an appropriate form of one of the words given below to complete the numbered sentences that follow. Two of the words have been used twice.

ALIENATE	FATHOM
BATTERY	FIT IN WITH
BRING OUT	FLUID
CONCOMITANT	OPT FOR
CONVEY	OUTCOME
DERIVE	PRAGMATIC
DISCORD	SUBSEQUENT

1. Precisely why so many of us ________________________ such great pleasure from wonderful music remains a true enigma.

2. The board of directors essentially cast all previous arguments aside and adopted a very ________________________ approach by conducting a cost / benefit analysis.

3. We were provided with a wide array of high-tech equipment to choose from in completing the commissioned landscape photographic series, but in the end we ________________________ a traditional 4x5-inch film camera because of the superior image quality and flexibility.

4. Both husband and wife expressed quite ________________________ views on their respective roles in caring for the children, and this naturally led to frequent heated arguments.

5. Studies have shown that immigrants who were extremely successful in their home countries often experience the greatest emotional problems in trying to ________________ and adapt to the new host society.

6. ________________________ to our last meeting, a number of new developments have made our previous decisions rather untenable.

7. The mellifluous ________________________ of his speech was matched only by his astounding range of vocabulary and his perfect pronunciation.

8. Standard practice in most business and professional environments is the written ________________________ of congratulatory remarks when an employee is promoted into a higher position.

9. The court will inform us of the ________________________ of the trial as soon as the jury has completed its deliberations.

10. For many people, the boundaries between justified suspicion and outright jealousy are quite ________________________.

11. Even Albert Einstein found certain conclusions that resulted from the equations of quantum physics difficult to ________________________, leading him to quip that God did not play dice.

12. People who have spent most of their lives in one type of culture often feel a deep sense of ________________________ when forced by circumstances to immigrate into a completely different type of culture and language environment.

13. Standardized language proficiency tests normally consist of an extensive ________________________ of components designed to measure an individual's communicative competence in several key skill areas.

14. ________________________ with the increased use of English in all types of global business, academic, and research environments has been a growing demand for competent one-on-one, highly individualized instruction.

15. Concert halls with expertly designed acoustical properties usually ________________________ the best in all musicians.

16. Emotionally disturbed children often experience great difficulty in ________________________ their thoughts, opinions, and feelings to others.

PART C

LANGUAGE FOCUS

1. Identify the noun clauses found in paragraph F. [For a review of NOUN CLAUSES, see the APPENDIX, section B.]

2. In paragraph M, identify gerunds used as subjects of sentences or clauses. [For a review of GERUNDS and INFINITIVES, see the APPENDIX, section C.]

3. In paragraphs B–F, identify fixed collocations of verbs / adjectives + prepositions. [For a review of COLLOCATIONS, see the APPENDIX, section D.]

4. Identify the infinitives of purpose in paragraph H.

5. What word(s) could we use to replace the word "it" at the beginning of paragraph M?

Sentence Transformation

For questions 6–10, use the word given below the first sentence to complete the second sentence in the blanks provided. Use between three and eight words including the given word. The given word must NOT be changed in any way, and the meaning of the sentences should be as similar as possible.

Example: We eagerly await a renewed encounter with you in the future.
forward
We are really <u>looking forward to seeing</u> you again in the future.

6. My instincts tell me we're going the wrong way.
gut
I have ______________________________ we're going the wrong way.

7. Janet studied both the piano and the flute, but she was more accomplished on the flute.
home
Janet studied both the piano and the flute, but she ______________ ______________ with the flute.

8. Even at a very early age, Midori displayed extraordinary musical talent.

   knack

   Even at a very early age, Midori had ______________________________ music.

9. This project is going to be exceptionally difficult and will require your total commitment.

   cut

   You're certainly going to have your ______________________________ with this project.

10. We need to avoid any further intradepartmental strife.

    steer

    We need ____ any further intradepartmental strife.

ULTIMATE CHALLENGE

PART D

Sentence Reconstruction

Reconstruct the following ten sentences by putting the individual words back into their correct order. All of the sentences represent TRUE statements that can be inferred from the information presented in the reading text. Supply appropriate punctuation as needed.

1. of to as and the many weaknesses use their tests employees companies personality MBTI the such identify strengths

   ____

   ____

   ____

2. of of of traits types a pairs Jung his four fundamental psychological around constructed theory framework

   ____

   ____

   ____

3. to the of over extroverts stimulation that tend more favor atmosphere lack subdued lively gatherings environments social

____

____

____

4. the a to for often given most candidate employ profiles suitable personality headhunters find position

____

____

____

5. of the the on largely type five relies obtained sensing through personality information senses

____

____

____

6. the the an to on all often inner conclusions relying personality seems instinct before reaches what intuiting be pertinent has presented been evidence

____

____

____

7. an a to to in be that appear counterparts adapted requires their marketing fast to sales better environment paced pitch aggressive extroverts contrast

____

____

____

8. be to to use members partners dating profiles best deemed online match personality fits services with

____

____

____

9. and to for of are often assignments companies which specific personality employees types organizations best use suited determine tests

____

____

____

10. in in are some behavior more than specific others patterns often readily cultures accepted

____

____

____

LANGUAGE IN USE

PART E

I Suggested Questions for Discussion

A. Why do some people seem to "hit it off" or "click" the instant they meet, while others seem to take an instant dislike to each other? Describe an experience you may have had with either (or both) of these extremes.

B. Should employees whose personalities are dramatically different be required to work together? Or, rather, should HR managers / directors / team leaders make an effort to find a suitable "match" for each individual?

C. Describe your own MBTI type. Based on your personal experience, do you get along better with someone who is similar to you, or do you prefer to be with someone who is quite different from you? Describe your experiences with each alternative.

II Suggested Questions for Written Research Projects

A. Conduct an online survey among your friends, classmates, or other groups of volunteers.

First, ask the participants to provide you with their own four-letter MBTI type.

Second, design a research question of interest to you with an appropriate questionnaire to submit to the same respondents who provided you with their MBTI types. Test to see whether there are any identifiable correlations between respondents' MBTI types and their responses to your questionnaire. Research questions might include, for example:

- ✦ Are you open to taking risks, or do you consider yourself to be risk-averse?
- ✦ At what time of day would you prefer to go for a walk?
- ✦ How often do you text your friends and family per day?
- ✦ How often do you call your friends and family?
- ✦ What is the maximum amount of time you would want to go without talking on the phone?
- ✦ Do you prefer shopping online or going to a traditional brick-and-mortar store?

Finally, write a report describing the purpose of your study, the methods you employed, the results you obtained, and whether you found any significant correlation between MBTI type and the answers you received to your questionnaire.

B. What are the advantages and disadvantages of being an introvert or an extrovert?

C. Describe and outline your own topic-related research question.

UNIT 3

DIFFERENT STROKES FOR DIFFERENT FOLKS

BEFORE YOU READ

Describe a few of the differences you have noticed between the culture you come from and other cultures you may have experienced, either through travel or through literature, television, or cinema.

DIRECTIONS: As you read the following text, fill in the numbered blanks with ONE suitable word.

CLOZE TASK

A Just as there are distinct types of personalities, there are also different types of human societies. U.S. American anthropologist Edward T. Hall (1981) described a number of the cultures he observed in terms of the forms of interaction the members of given societies engaged in, as well as the types of relationships typical of and expected within those cultures. Particularly noteworthy was Hall's distinction between high-context and low-context cultures (see also Hall & Hall, 1990).

B In high-context countries such as Japan and Korea, [1]__________ the form and the content of communication are highly dependent on and correlated [2]____________________ essential background information pertaining to the age, gender, social position, or status of the interlocutors. Interpersonal relationships evolve over a long period of time or are often not even possible because of the vast differences that may [3]__________ between individuals in terms of the factors cited above. In Korean society, for example, the age and social position of two given speakers co-determine the words, verb forms, and overall lexico-grammatical / lexico-pragmatic character of the sentences the speakers are permitted to use.

C The elaborate and extensive systems of honorific forms common to both Japanese and Korean [4]__________________ exceptional demands on the non-native speaker who is attempting to learn [5]______________ languages. Numerous levels of hierarchy or formality that govern lexical choice, word form, and syntax must first be internalized before the learner attempts to debut her [6]____________________ in public. Even the seemingly most innocuous and mundane statements about the weather may be unwittingly rendered in an offensive form.

D In Japan, most speakers are aware of the important [7]__________ between *honne* (literally a person's true feelings) and *tatemae*, a façade required for proper public conduct. The private, individual feelings, wants, and opinions of a speaker must traditionally take a back seat to the overall harmony of the group or society [8]______________ large. Peer pressure to conform to the norms of the group is enormously powerful; failure to conform may mean unwanted ostracism from many levels of society. One common Japanese adage warns that the nail that sticks out gets hammered down. Conformity is achieved by means of often tacit rules that govern many aspects of conduct in daily life. At the workplace, for example, employees are expected—and hence required—to remain in the office until the boss has left, [9]____________________ if there is no such clause in whatever form of written contract that might exist.

Image production credit: iStock.com/btrenkel

E Such extreme forms of "respect" and context-dependent adherence to norms might be utterly unthinkable to someone [10]________________ mindset is deeply [11]________________________ in the low-context societal norms of Germany, the Netherlands, or Scotland. A Berliner working in Tokyo might simply pack [12]________________________ her belongings at 5 p.m. and head for the door. She might counter the chastising glares with a glance at her watch and the verbal update: "My contract says my working hours are from 9 a.m. to 5 p.m., and by my watch, it's 5. See you tomorrow!" That is, if there is a tomorrow for her. Such behavior is common and expected in low-context societies simply because many aspects of individual conduct are codified in and sanctioned by contracts, which legally supersede any personal feelings of respect or obligation.

F It is readily [13]________________________ that these opposite types of culture strongly affect the norms and styles of communication shared by the individuals living within a given society. The language mastered by individuals in high-context societies is often carefully weighed and may only indirectly imply a hidden subtextual value. In [14]_____________, the discourse patterns commonly found in many low-context countries may be quite blunt to the [15]______________ of appearing rude, although the speakers harbor perhaps no hostile intentions at [16]________________.

G In a rather humorous article addressing the seemingly irreconcilable [17]________________________ between German directness and British manners, Stephen Evans (2011) of *BBC News* noted that the German owners of BMW were initially at a loss to understand the communication style of the English managers [18]________________________ the German parent company acquired the British carmaker Rover. The English tend to cloak their messages in nice little packages of euphemistic indirectness to make the message easier to swallow. One could easily imagine an English gentleman commenting to another as the ship they're sailing on takes on water: "There seems to be a bit of a problem here. I'd say this calls for another gin and tonic."

H As Professor Juliane House of the University of Hamburg noted, the Germans don't even have an expression for "small talk," because they consider it "empty verbiage." As Evans noted, the German translation of the popular English children's story, *A Bear Called Paddington*, completely omitted the friendly chit-chat that Paddington Bear was [19]__________ in with Mrs. Bird when the two [20]____________________ into each other at the train station. Germans don't do small talk, and hence any translation of the congenial niceties would have been meaningless.

I Other aspects of culture [21]____________________ as collectivist versus individualist traditions, and perceptions of distance to figures of power and seats of authority also greatly influence the styles of communication that characterize the norms of many ethnic and linguistic groups. Individuals in low power-distance cultures tend to believe that they are able to effect fundamental changes within the society, regardless of who is in power; whereas in high power-distance societies, citizens tend to think that they are powerless to bring about any type of change, because those in seats of authority command overwhelming power to resist all efforts to change the existing system. Moreover, differences in communication styles [22] __________________ even exist within the same culture. U.S. American linguist Deborah Tannen (1990), whose [23]______________ of interethnic and gender-based differences in communication patterns have received critical acclaim, noted for example the sharp distinctions in intended meaning in the opinions expressed by northerners (e.g., people from New York, Philadelphia, Boston) and southerners in the United States. The statement, "I don't really know her" when uttered by a New Yorker can be taken at face [24]____________________, with the intended meaning accurately reflected in just what the sentence says. When spoken by a southerner, however, [25]____________________ same sentence might imply a great deal of contempt and hostility on the [26] ______________ of the speaker toward "her."

J The globalization of international icons in film, television, and music has served [27]____________________ somewhat soften the sharp differences that continue to exist between cultures, but miscommunication and communication breakdowns also continue to occur on a daily basis as a [28]______________________ of both culture- and gender-based differences in communication styles. But nowhere is an acute awareness of the importance of culture more important than in global corporations. A growing [29]______________________ of research has pointed to the enormous significance of cultural differences in managerial disputes and negotiation processes (Adair & Brett, 2005; Chaisrakeo & Speece, 2004; Gibson, 1998; Graham, 1983; Graham, Kim, Lin & Robinson, 1988; Simintiras & Thomas, 1998), approaches to conflict resolution (Chua & Gudykunst, 1987), contractual agreements among multinational firms (Guzzo & Noonan, 1994; Karacay-Aydin, 2009), and overall employee perceptions and job satisfaction (Thomas, Kevin & Ravlin, 2003) in the global business context.

K Nguyen, Heeler & Taran (2007) were able to show that even the pricing strategies [30]______________________ by companies in order to attract a larger number of customers vary significantly in their effects. Consumers in high-context cultures tend to favor price endings that are even (e.g., $500.00), whereas buyers in low-context cultures are often attracted to the psychological effect created by uneven price endings ($499.99). According to the authors of the [31]______________________, consumers "in high-context, non-Western cultures may be less prone to the illusion of cheapness or gain created by odd endings, and more likely offended by such perceived attempts to 'fool' them" (Nguyen, Heeler & Taran, 2007, p. 206). Other studies have confirmed the importance of culture-based perceptions of numbers and of psychological attitudes associated with [32]______________________ perceptions (Diller & Brielmaier, 1995; Kreul, 1982; Lip, 1992; Poltrock & Schwartz, 1984; Schindler, 2001).

L Würtz (2005) examined the differences prevalent in the use of visual effects in online marketing campaigns for the American fast-food giant McDonald's. By [33]______________________ the advertising images found in representative high-context (Japan, China, and Korea) and low-context (Germany, Denmark, Sweden, Norway, Finland, USA) societies, she confirmed the contrasting communication styles outlined by numerous previous studies. In addition, Würtz was able to corroborate the link previously posited by Hofstede (1984, 1996) between high-context and collectivist societies on [34]____________________ one hand and low-context and individualist societies on the other. The advertising campaigns featured on the McDonald's websites in high-context cultures tended to emphasize the family- or group-based outing to the fast-food restaurant, [35]____________________ the low-context versions featured particularly young individuals in blissful isolation, completely absorbed in their own pleasures, such as with music streaming from an iPod while downing their favorite French fries or hamburger. An awareness of [36]______________ these important differences play into the overall success or [37] ____________________ of marketing efforts would be critical to all multinational corporations (Tse, Lee, Vertinsky & Wehrung, 1988).

M Global enterprises are increasingly reliant on transplant employees who are required to work for the company abroad. When the employee's own cultural values clash with those of the new environment, psychological problems can ensue. Andrew L. Molinsky (2013) of Brandeis University has called this difficult process of adaptation across societal frameworks "cultural retooling." According to Molinsky, successfully adapting "to the norms of a new culture helps avoid the negative repercussions of culturally inappropriate behavior and its associated stereotypes [...]. It also increases the likelihood of fitting in, winning the respect and admiration of foreign colleagues, and being an effective and persuasive collaborator on a cross-cultural team [...]."

N As corporations, associations, and individuals [38]______________ their horizons beyond the confines of their own regional settings and domestic spheres of influence, an even greater understanding of the role [39]____________________ by cultures in shaping our perceptions of the world and in framing the manner in [40]____________________ we relate to each other will be needed. But we have only barely begun to open up the layers of cultural influence on the forms of interaction we engage in with each other. As "global citizens," we are, in many ways, becoming more similar to each other. We may one day conclude that certain key differences should be maintained and treasured.

REFERENCES

Adair, W. L. & Brett, J. M. (2005). The negotiation dance: Time, culture, and behavioral sequences in negotiation. *Organization Science, 16*, 33–51.

Chaisrakeo, S. & Speece, M. (2004). Culture, intercultural communication competence, and sales negotiation: A qualitative research approach. *Journal of Business & Industrial Marketing, 19*(4), 267–282.

Chua, E. G. & Gudykunst, W. B. (1987). Conflict resolution styles in low- and high-context cultures. *Communication Research Reports, 4*, 32–37.

Diller, H. & Brielmaier, A. (1995). The impact of rounding-up odd prices: Results of a field experiment in German drugstores. *Pricing Strategy & Practice, 3*(4), 4–13.

Evans, S. (2011, May 26). What Paddington tells us about German v British manners. BBC News. Retrieved November 9, 2014 from http://www.bbc.co.uk/news/world-europe-13545386

Gibson, C. B. (1998). Do you hear what I hear: A framework for reconciling intercultural communication difficulties arising from cognitive styles and cultural values. In P. C. Barley & M. Erez (Eds.). *New perspectives on international industrial/organizational psychology*. (pp. 335-362). San Francisco, CA: The New Lexington Press.

Graham, J. L. (1983). Business negotiation in Japan, Brazil and the United States. *Journal of International Business Studies, 14*(1), 47–62.

Graham, J. L., Kim, D. K., Lin, C. Y. & Robinson, M. (1988). Buyer-seller negotiation around the Pacific Rim: Differences in fundamental exchange processes. *Journal of Consumer Research, 15*, 48–54.

Guzzo, R. A. & Noonan, K. A. (1994). Human resource practices as communications and the psychological contract. *Human Resource Management, 33*, 447–462.

Hall, E., (1976). *Beyond culture*. New York: Doubleday.

Hall, E. & Hall, M. R. (1990). *Understanding cultural differences*. Yarmouth, ME: Intercultural Press Inc.

Hofstede, G. (1984). *Culture's consequences: International differences in work-related attitudes*. Beverly Hills, CA: Sage Publications.

Hofstede, G. (1996). *Cultures and organizations, software of the mind: Intercultural cooperation and its importance for survival.* New York: McGraw-Hill.

Karacay-Aydin, G. (2009). Third-party roles in mediating or preventing psychological contract violations in high-context cultures. *The Business Review, 12*(1), 167–173.

Kreul, L. M. (1982). Magic numbers: psychological effects of menu pricing. *Cornell Hotel and Restaurant Administration Quarterly, 23*(2), 70–75.

Lip, E. (1992). *Chinese numbers: Significance, symbolism and traditions.* Singapore: Times Book International.

Molinsky, A. L. (2013). The psychological processes of cultural retooling. *Academy of Management Journal.* Retrieved November 16, 2014 from http://dx.doi.org/10.5465/amj.2010.0492

Nguyen, A., Heeler, R. M. & Taran, Z. (2007). High-low context cultures and price-ending practices. *Journal of Product & Brand Management, 16*(3), 206–214.

Poltrock, S. E. & Schwartz, D. R. (1984). Comparative judgments of multidigit numbers. *Journal of Experimental Psychology: Learning, Memory, and Cognition, 10*, 32–45.

Schindler, R. M. (2001). Price level of 99-ending prices: image versus reality. *Marketing Letters, 82*(1), 239–242.

Simintiras, A. C. & Thomas, A. H. (1998). Cross-cultural sales negotiations: A literature review and research propositions. *International Marketing Review, 15*(1), 10–28.

Tannen, D. (1990). Ethnic style in male-female conversation. In J. J. Gumperz (Ed.) *Language and Social Identity.* (pp. 220–232). Cambridge, UK: Cambridge University Press.

Thomas, D. C., Au, K. & Ravlin, E. C. (2003). Cultural variation and the psychological contract. *Journal of Organizational Behavior, 24*(5), 451–471.

Tse, D. K., Lee, K., Vertinsky, I. & Wehrung, D. A. (1988). Does culture matter? A cross-cultural study of executives' choice, decisiveness, and risk adjustment in international marketing. *Journal of Marketing, 52*, 81–95.

Würtz, E. (2005). A cross-cultural analysis of websites from high-context cultures and low-context cultures. *Journal of Computer-Mediated Communication.* Retrieved November 13, 2014 from http://jcmc.indiana.edu/vol11/issue1/wuertz.html

POST-READING QUESTIONS

1. How did your views of your own culture change after reading the text?
2. Which other cultures around the world is your own most similar to and in what ways?
3. What are some of the difficulties you might have if you lived in a culture that is very different from your own?
4. Which other culture would you most like to explore and why?
5. Is it better to be direct at the risk of hurting another's feelings, or to leave things "implied"? Why?
6. Describe the key differences between high- and low-context cultures.
7. Explain the difference between individualist and collectivist societies.
8. In your own words, explain how cultural backgrounds impact the communication styles of speakers.

VOCABULARY WORK

PART A

From the reading text, find the words or phrases that have similar meanings to the words / phrases given in the numbered lists below. The first one has been done for you as an example.

From Paragraphs A–G:	Synonymous Word or Phrase
1. germane to; relevant to; appertaining to	<u>pertaining to (paragraph B)</u>
2. pretense; mask; front	________________
3. authorized; permitted; legalized	________________
4. duty; responsibility	________________
5. common; everyday; routine; normal	________________
6. displace; supplant; override; overrule	________________
7. conveying respect and esteem; forms used to show respect	________________
8. associated with; corresponding with; connected with	________________

9. without purpose or intention; accidentally; inadvertently ____________________
10. exile; expulsion; banishment; ouster ____________________
11. harmless; inoffensive ____________________
12. formalized; summarized in legal code ____________________
13. speakers in conversation ____________________
14. evasiveness; obliqueness; implicitness ____________________
15. personal effects; personal property ____________________
16. angry stares; scowls ____________________
17. at first ____________________
18. develop over time ____________________
19. unspoken; undeclared; unstated ____________________
20. frank; candid; outspoken ____________________
21. aggressive; belligerent; antagonistic ____________________
22. provision in law or written document; section of legal document ____________________
23. to cover; to shroud; to veil; to disguise; to conceal ____________________
24. gauged; considered; contemplated; deliberated ____________________

From Paragraphs H–N: Synonymous Word or Phrase

25. praise; ovation; celebration ____________________
26. graces; little pleasures; trivialities ____________________
27. controversies; strife; conflicts; debates ____________________
28. idle talk; small talk ____________________
29. sharp; intense; penetrating; keen; incisive ____________________

30. as per written agreement or legal document ____________________

31. overpowering; staggering; crushing; irresistible ____________________

32. images; idols ____________________

VOCABULARY WORK

PART B

Choose an appropriate form of one of the words given below to complete the numbered sentences that follow. Two of the words have been used twice.

CLAUSE	INITIAL
CODIFY	INNOCUOUS
CONTRACT	OBLIGE
CORRELATE	SANCTION
DISPUTE	SUPERSEDE
EVOLVE	TACIT
ICON	WEIGH

1. We refer again to the ____________________ and primacy of international maritime law over corporate regulations.

2. The proposed amendments to the organization's charter have not yet been ____________________ by the board of governors, but their approval is expected within the week.

3. I simply mentioned, quite ____________________ I thought, that Alice had put on a few extra pounds, at which point she threw the red wine in my face.

4. Discovered by accident, Vivian Maier's ____________________ black and white images of American street life fascinate through both their pictorial narrative and the naturalness of the subjects she chose to depict.

5. In the hands of highly skilled performance musicians, musical instruments often ____________________ into what seems to be a natural extension of the performer's body and mind.

6. We still need more time to carefully ________________________ the costs versus benefits of the project for our department.

7. By remaining silent throughout the prosecutor's questioning, Maria ________________________ acknowledged that her husband had committed the crime.

8. The regulations approved by the World Trade Organization in this matter ________________________ all previously existing national statutes.

9. Although nothing was formalized in writing or in an actual verbal agreement, the ________________________ assumption after days of negotiation was that corporate headquarters would cover our additional charges, which they're now refusing to do.

10. What was ________________________ believed to be a severe cold actually turned out to be viral meningitis.

11. You are by no means ________________________ to take my advice; it's simply intended as a suggestion.

12. A rarely cited ________________________ in the state's penal code has been invoked to justify the severe punishment handed down by the court in its most recent case involving identity theft.

13. The country's entire tax system is ________________________ in a three-thousand-page opus.

14. International disagreements involving unfair trading practices and currency manipulation are now routinely brought before the World Trade Organization's ________________________ settlement body.

15. I'm afraid you are ________________________ obliged to work every fifth Monday evening until 7:30 in addition to your regular 40-hour week.

16. Early childhood exposure to an avid reading environment is highly ________________________ with later success in all areas of life.

LANGUAGE FOCUS

PART C

1. Identify instances of grammatical parallelism in paragraphs A–C.

2. In paragraphs A–G, identify sentences that begin with prepositional phrases.

3. Identify the adverb clauses in paragraphs D–H and specify the type of adverb clauses used (e.g., causality, purpose, contrast, condition, etc.) [For a review of ADVERB CLAUSES, see the APPENDIX, section B.]

4. In paragraph I, locate two reduced adverb clauses.

5. What antecedent noun does the pronoun "she" refer to in the phrase "She might counter the chastising …" (paragraph E)?

Sentence Transformation

For questions 6–10, use the word given below the first sentence to complete the second sentence in the blanks provided. Use between three and eight words including the given word. The given word must NOT be changed in any way, and the meaning of the sentences should be as similar as possible.

Example: We eagerly await a renewed encounter with you in the future.
forward
We are really <u>looking forward to seeing</u> you again in the future.

6. Indra was the only daughter among five children, so her parents always gave priority to her brothers' wants and needs.
   seat
   Because Indra was the only daughter among five children, her own wants and needs always ______________________________ to her brothers'.

7. The measures taken by the county government are unprecedented and demand an emergency meeting of the board of supervisors.
   call
   The unprecedented measures taken by the county government ________ ______________________________ emergency meeting of the board of supervisors.

8. When you're shopping for a new car, don't be fooled by cheap sales gimmicks.
   taken
   Don't allow yourself ______________________________ cheap sales gimmicks when you're shopping for a new car.

9. Monica and her husband frequently disagree over what type of food is best for their children.
   odds
   Monica and her husband are frequently ______________________ the best type of food to give their children.

10. When the largest donors pulled out their pledged funding, the project failed immediately.
    fell
    The project ______________________________ after the largest donors withdrew their pledged support.

PART D

ULTIMATE CHALLENGE

Sentence Reconstruction

Reconstruct the following ten sentences by putting the individual words back into their correct order. All of the sentences represent TRUE statements that can be inferred from the information presented in the reading text. Supply appropriate punctuation as needed.

1. in in to be than context low those cultures found context high styles far communication explicit tend less societies

   ____

   ____

   ____

2. a in is as to can be very Berlin typical appear direct speech city everyday low patterns which described context

____

____

____

3. in between by are written and low relations contracts cultures context largely employers determined employees

____

____

____

4. a in evolve cultures context relationships over normally time high long

____

____

____

5. in by or of are norms context codes individuals less low tacit conduct bound societies

____

____

____

6. in in or of before a the situation range individuals speaking relations must like given entire Japan involved consider countries acting

____

____

____

7. to to the the on ice small tend between rely individuals English talk break

____

____

____

8. in in to about they low that distance people able desired feel power society bring changes are often cultures

____

____

____

9. a of or in in the members individual high advertising family context setting cultures campaigns group often place friends

____

____

____

10. of to the the have in multinational mediated corporations workplace importance started culturally styles global enormous communication recognize

____

____

____

PART E

LANGUAGE IN USE

I Suggested Questions for Discussion

A. Describe your own culture. Is it high or low context? What importance does your culture place on the freedom of the individual as opposed to the wants and needs of the collective society as a whole?

B. In what ways does your culture stress, or ignore, personal boundaries? What is the attitude in your country about individuals' stopping by a friend's house without an invitation? What kinds of topics are considered taboo or impolite in your culture? Is there an appropriate translation in your language for the idiomatic "TMI" ("too much information") in English?

C. Who is expected to take care of aging parents when they are no longer able to care for themselves? How do older parents feel about living with their own children?

II Suggested Questions for Written Research Projects

A. Identify noteworthy shifts in cultural attitudes in your country and provide plausible explanations for why these changes have occurred.

B. Discuss the advantages and disadvantages of collectivist versus individualist societies.

C. Describe and outline your own topic-related research question.

ENGLISH AS THE GLOBAL LINGUA FRANCA

UNIT 4

BEFORE YOU READ

Have you ever been in a country in which you were completely unable to communicate with anyone? How did you overcome the difficulties involved in this situation? Does your own country have an official national language?

DIRECTIONS: As you read the following text, complete the blanks after the numbered brackets with an appropriate form of the word given in capital letters. The first one has been done for you as an example.

CLOZE TASK

A In his 2010 book [0] TITLE <u>titled</u> *Globish: How the English Language Became the World's Language*, author Robert McCrum [1] LIKE_____________ the global character of the English language to that of a standardized computer [2] PROGRAM_____________ language; neither is the prerogative or exclusive property of the country in which it was developed. Instead, both are used by vast numbers of individuals around the world for a multitude of purposes.

B English, or "Globish," has become the de facto standard tool of communication in international trade, finance, science, technology, transportation, and [3] DIPLOMAT_____________. The reasons for this exalted status are multifaceted. The British Empire successfully spread the use of English throughout its former colonies, which today include the 54 nations that constitute the Commonwealth, including such giants as Bangladesh, India, Nigeria, and Pakistan. The economic, scientific, and technological strength of the United States after World War II served to [4] SOLID____________ the role of English in international trade and commerce—on land, on the seas, and in the air. The growth and expansion of leading universities in the United States as centers of cutting-edge research and as attractors for large [5] ENDOW____________ with promising careers for worthy scholars further supported the consolidation of English as the now dominant language of international scholarship.

C By the early 1990s, 88.6% of all peer-reviewed articles in science and technology were published in English. In 1987, *The Scientist* noted that academics who do not know English face two enormous obstacles to serious research. First, they are unable to use the vast [6] MAJOR________ of studies germane to their own undertakings because most peer-reviewed publications appear in English. Second, the research published by scientists who have not mastered English is likely to go completely [7] NOTICE ________________ by the global community of scholars. It is simply too daunting a task for most human minds to acquire a high level of proficiency in even one foreign language; attempting the same in the dozens of languages that are the native tongues of the collective body of scientists and academics worldwide borders on the impossible.

D But there is one other factor related to the language itself that helps to explain the primary position English enjoys among larger and smaller [8] COMPETE________________. When compared to those languages considered by the U.S. Foreign Service Institute to be "extraordinarily difficult" to master, English is indeed a piece of cake.

E All languages are highly dynamic, in permanent processes of change and [9] ADAPT____________. As linguist John McWhorter (2002) has noted, [10] COMPLEX____________ is a characteristic that applies to all human languages; however, this does not mean that all languages are equally complex. The great number of neighboring language groups that affected the structural development of English over the last 2,000 years has also led to a more streamlined character of the language in distinct contrast to the vast majority of its Indo-European and non-Indo-European counterparts (Baugh & Cable, 1978). English has largely eliminated the extraordinarily complex verb systems that are characteristic of highly inflecting languages like Sanskrit, Hindi/Urdu, and Classical Greek. For all practical purposes, English has also largely done away with inherent reflexive markers (cf. the English version of "I remember" with the German ("I remember myself" (*ich erinnere mich*), or the French (*je me souviens*), the complex noun declension systems, and required evidential markings in languages like Tseze. (Evidential markings are [11] GRAMMAR ______________ elements that give the [12] RECEIVE______________ of a message a clear indication of how the content of the statement was obtained or learned. Most languages provide indicators of such information, but in a number of languages, this is an obligatory component of speech.) Of equal importance for the learner, English has also dispensed with the quite unnecessary gender [13] CLASS______________ of all nouns found in European and in a wide spectrum of other languages as well (e.g., in German, a spoon is masculine (*der Löffel*), a fork is feminine (*die Gabel*), and a knife is neuter (*das Messer*)). The learner of English need not bother with having to [14] MEMORY______________ the gender associated with every known noun on earth.

Image production credit: iStock.com/StockFinland

F The English writing system is also much easier to master when compared with the written forms of many other world languages. Mandarin Chinese, with by far the largest number of native speakers of any language, has more than 50,000 characters, each depicting a separate concept. Mastering even a fraction of these characters requires many years of dedicated study and consistent practice. And with respect to spoken Chinese, even for the learner who is already acquainted with basic vocabulary, [15] CIPHER__________________ the quick barrage of possible tone combinations that determine the meaning of each word is in itself a formidably difficult task. Each word in Mandarin (and in all other Chinese dialects) is distinguished by one of several tone combinations, with countless numbers of homophones forming the basic lexical units. Depending on the tone used in any given context, the meaning of a given word or phrase can vary [16] DRAMA__________________. The anxious listener who is confronted with the rapid-fire [17] SUCCEED__________ of words and tones might have to decide on the fly whether the speaker said she wanted to take a nap or eat water dumplings.

G Most business [18] EXECUTE_____________ and research scientists can gain an excellent working command of English in the same amount of time that would barely allow them to advance into an intermediate level in Mandarin. Considering the pressing obligations to publish, to advance research, and/or to expand a company's corporate profits, most professionals simply don't have the thousands of hours of extra time needed to master such a difficult language. Add to this the fact that Mandarin is still largely restricted to eastern Asia itself and to isolated Chinese ethnic communities scattered throughout various world metropolises, and it seems unlikely that the dominance of English will be seriously challenged within the [19] FORESEE_____________ future, at least not by Mandarin.

H Arabic presents other extraordinary challenges for those attempting to master the language. In essence, every learner of Arabic needs to become diglossic, meaning to master two separate languages. Modern "Standard" Arabic, the highest form of Arabic based on the Koran, serves to unite the most educated Arabic speakers all over the world, and it is the target language for the vast majority of learners. At the same time, each region of the Arab world speaks its own "dialect," which is learned at home in the family and is essentially a separate language from the Modern Standard Arabic taught in the school system. Depending on the degree of [20]

GEOGRAPHY ____________________ separation involved, these regional dialects are often mutually unintelligible.

I In all its forms, Arabic challenges even the most gifted of language learners with an [21] EXCEPT____________ complex grammatical system based on lexical roots of three consonants (e.g. k–t–b for all things involving writing: *katib* = a writer, *kataba* = he wrote, *kutub* = books). This difficulty is enhanced by the fact that many vowels are not written out so that the learner often must guess from context which form of the root system fits into a given place within the sentence.

J Other languages such as Hindi and Urdu, with hundreds of millions of both native and second-language speakers have equally demanding and complex grammar systems. But with 40 consonants that must be carefully formed in specific parts of the mouth so as to distinguish between hundreds of words that sound almost exactly the same to Western ears, these languages also present vexing phonological problems for all learners from non-related language groups.

K A brief [22] COMPARE____________ between English and the majority of other languages commonly encountered at international conferences should suffice to convince even die-hard skeptics of the clear advantages of using English as the world's language. Already, on any given day in this global arena of instant messaging, tweets, and cell phone calls, English-based interactions among non-native speakers outnumber those conducted by native speakers by a wide margin, by some estimates as much as three to one. India's growing middle class is already highly proficient in English, as the language serves as a unifying medium of interaction among the country's hundreds of regional dialects.

L China's highly [23] EFFECT____________ efforts to teach its young the language of global trade and science have resulted in untold numbers of highly proficient speakers and writers of English, often at levels on par with those of educated native speakers. China's Li Yang, founder of Crazy English, put it best with the slogan: Conquer English to Make China Strong (McCrum, 2010, p. 252). China is doing just that. In the not-too-distant future, China may in fact become the country with the largest number of English speakers—albeit as speakers of English as a second language—[24] PASS____________ the numbers currently held by India and the United States in the top positions.

M Non-native speakers of English are often puzzled by the strong [25] REGION______________________ of the language's varied [26] PRONOUNCE__________________ patterns. Even within the countries that constitute the United Kingdom, regional accents vary enormously and are often extremely difficult for people from other regions to understand. In the early days of radio, the accepted "standard" of spoken British English became a cultivated accent that later carried the moniker "Received Pronunciation"—or RP. This posh-sounding pronunciation was in fact not the product of a regional influence as such, but rather a cultivated and acquired pronunciation pattern popular within the "public school" (termed "private schools" in the USA) system at the time. Like many other aspects of life in the United Kingdom, Received Pronunciation was also frequently associated with a certain social status, usually the upper-middle class. But that accent has largely disappeared in the UK, especially among the younger generation. Close scrutiny of the Queen's radio addresses over the years shows that she, too, has adapted her pronunciation patterns to the changing times.

N But British accents particularly within England itself are still strongly class oriented. Working-class accents are often noticeable by the absence of an aspirated "h," especially in the traditional Cockney dialect, and the double "t" in words such as "butter" or "bottle" becomes a consonant sound almost akin to a glottal stop. In addition, the greater the regional influence on any given accent, the greater the likelihood that the speaker will have problems communicating successfully with compatriots from regions much farther away. Scottish, Geordie, Cornwall, Lancashire, and Nottinghamshire dialects of English might be difficult to understand for someone who has grown up surrounded exclusively by an upper-class accent. In fact, the speaker of the higher social class is likely to have much more in common with her American counterpart from Washington, D. C.

than she is with someone from the Highlands of Scotland. It might be noted that Americans tend to believe that any British accent sounds "posh"—a view most certainly not held in the UK itself.

O Even though American accents are less class-specific than their English counterparts are, the United States is also characterized by fairly strong regional influences that determine pronunciation patterns. In areas such as rural Maine, there is often evidence of the original Scandinavian influence in the spoken language of many of the residents, particularly in the patterns of supra-segmentals. In Brooklyn, a borough of New York City, many vowel sounds are strongly affected by Russian, Yiddish, and Italian [27] MIGRATE_____________ who lent their own particular flavor to the English they adopted over time. The Brooklyn "o" in "coffee," for example, tends to sound like "oy" as in the Yiddish word for non-Jews, "goyim." In addition to their distinct "drawl," which causes many vowel sounds to be voiced as multiple diphthongs in series, rural Southerners often use terms that strike Americans from other regions of the country as being thoroughly antiquated or archaic. Such lexical anachronisms in American English, evident in the [28] WIDE_______________ use of words like "road" instead of "street," "reckon" instead of "think," or "pail" instead of "bucket" are most likely the result of the fairly homogeneous British influence that dominated the South in the seventeenth century. Other important regions of the English-speaking world exhibit their own distinct pronunciation patterns, often making the residents easily identifiable as New Zealanders, Australians, Scots, South Africans, Jamaicans, or Indians (Wells, 1982).

P In light of what seems to be the very [29] REGION_____________ character of English as the global language, the question naturally arises as to what "the" standard should be. Young learners of English as a second or foreign language often become quite frustrated in their attempts to sound exactly like this or that native speaker they might admire, be that a pop singer, sports icon, or famous movie star. There are, however, vast differences in individual ability and [30] MOTIVE_________________ (Moyer, 2008) among all learners, with some acquiring near native speaker-like pronunciation in a very short time. Many learners quite naturally acquire the regional pronunciation patterns of the English speakers with whom they spend most of their time. But most instructors of English around the world realize that "perfect" pronunciation should not and cannot be the goal in language instruction. Rather, excellent [31] INTELLIGENT ______________________ in all practical circumstances should guide both instructor and learner (Jenkins, 2000, 2002; Kenworthy, 1987; Munro & Derwing, 1999). Radio, television, DVDs, and the Internet have all done their part to make the world—in linguistics terms at least—just a wee bit smaller, and the proof of this is in the hundreds of conferences and negotiation settings held annually in all parts of the globe, bringing together men and women from all walks of life, from all types of professional, political, academic, religious, and ethnic backgrounds, into forums of successful dialogue.

Q Today, the biggest problems emerging from the globalization of English as "the world's language" have to do with the culturally mediated communication styles highlighted in the previous unit. These differences—which can make or break a business deal, job interview, or marriage—encompass many important aspects of the way in which messages are conveyed and interpreted. These include (but are by no means limited to) the [32] WILL____________ or inability to tolerate long pauses or even extended silence during conversations (Ephratt, 2008, 2011; Jaworski, 1993, 2000; Saville-Troike, 1985; Tiersma, 1995); the extensive use of "small talk" to "break the ice" when strangers first meet versus the complete absence of such in certain cultural contexts (Beinstein, 1975; Coupland, 2003; Klein, 1993); the eagerness and "willingness to communicate" (MacIntyre, Doernyei, Clement & Noels, 1998; McCroskey, 1992; Yashima, 2002) versus a more reserved, reticent demeanor; the type and timing of multiple forms of "feedback" versus the paucity of such (Stubbe, 1997); and of course the paramount importance of paralinguistic features such as smiles, gestures, pitch, cadence, and volume in spoken [33] CHANGE_____________ (Anderson, 2006; Archer, 1997; LaFrance and Mayo, 1978; Roth, 2002).

R A [34] SUBSTANCE____________________ body of pragmatics research continues to stress the importance of all these facets of the communication process. Global success today requires good communication skills, which in turn assume an acute [35] AWARE____________ of the important differences found in contrasting cultural contexts (Crystal, 2003; Heydenfeldt, 2000). Classroom instruction in English has tended to shy away from addressing the pragmatic sides of language teaching, but experience informs us that pinpointing problem areas and actively devising strategies to [36] COME____________ these tricky barriers to successful communication are indeed the approach to be taken.

S Once again, the global business community has been leading the way in further consolidating the role of English as the world's lingua franca. According to a report published in a May 2012 issue of *Harvard Business Review*, increasing numbers of large multinational businesses are "mandating English as the common corporate language," often even within the company's home-country headquarters! These include such global giants as Airbus, Aventis, Daimler-Chrysler, Nestle, Rakuten, Renault, Samsung, and SAP, to name only a few. Many of these companies have embarked on very effective training programs in English to ensure that their higher-level employees with the greatest exposure to colleagues or clients from other language backgrounds can successfully meet the challenge by becoming proficient communicators in English.

T In an interview with Joe Castaldo of *Canadian Business*, Tsedal Neeley, the author of the HBR study, stressed that for "companies that have global aspirations, there's absolutely no choice."

REFERENCES

Anderson, M. (2006). Nonverbal communication. In: K. Brown (Ed.), *Encyclopedia of language and linguistics*, 2nd ed. (pp. 689–692). Amsterdam: Elsevier.

Archer, D. (1997). Unspoken diversity: Cultural differences in gestures. *Qualitative Sociology*, *20*(1), 79–105.

Baugh, A. C. & Cable, T. (1978). *A history of the English language*. Englewood Cliffs, NJ: Prentice-Hall.

Beinstein, J. (1975). Small talk as social gesture. *Journal of Communication*, *25*(4), 147–154.

Castaldo, J. (2012, March 14). English-only at multinationals can have negative consequences. *Canadian Business*. Retrieved July 26, 2014 from http://www.canadianbusiness.com/lifestyle/english-only-at-multinationals-can-have-negative-consequences/

Coupland, J. (2003). Small talk: Social functions. *Research on Language and Social Interaction, 36*(1), 1–6.

Crystal, D. (2003). *English as a global language*. Cambridge, UK: Cambridge University Press.

Ephratt, M. (2008). The functions of silence. *Journal of Pragmatics, 40*, 1909–1938.

Ephratt, M. (2011). Linguistic, paralinguistic and extralinguistic speech and silence. *Journal of Pragmatics, 43*, 2286–2307.

Heydenfeldt, J. G. (2000). The influence of individualism/collectivism on Mexican and US business negotiation. *International Journal of Intercultural Relations, 24*(3), 383-407.

Jaworski, A. (1993). *The power of silence: Social and pragmatic perspectives*. Newbury Park, CA: Sage.

Jaworski, A. (2000). Silence and small talk. In: J. Coupland (Ed.), *Small talk* (pp. 110–132). London: Longman.

Jenkins, J. (2000). *The phonology of English as an international language*. Oxford, UK: Oxford University Press.

Jenkins, J. (2002). A sociolinguistically based, empirically researched pronunciation syllabus for English as an international language. *Applied Linguistics, 23*(1), 87–103.

Kenworthy, J. (1987). Teaching English pronunciation. Oxford, UK: Oxford University Press.

Klein, N. (1993). Small talk as a learning goal in second-language instruction. *Beiträge zur Fremdsprachenvermittlung aus dem Konstanzer SLI, 25*, 54–68.

LaFrance, M. & Mayo, C. (1978). Cultural aspects of nonverbal communication. *International Journal of Intercultural Relations, 2*(1), 71–89.

MacIntyre, P. D., Doernyei, Z., Clement, R. & Noels, K. A. (1998). Conceptualizing willingness to communicate in an L2: A situational model of L2 confidence and affiliation. *The Modern Language Journal, 82*(4), 545–562.

McCroskey, J. C. (1992). Reliability and validity of the willingness to communicate scale. *Communication Quarterly, 40*(1), pp. 18–25.

McCrum, R. (2010). *Globish: How the English language became the world's language*. New York: W. W. Norton & Company.

McWhorter, J. (2002). *The power of Babel: A natural history of language*. New York: HarperCollins.

Moyer, A. (2008). Ultimate attainment in L2 phonology: The critical factors of age, motivation, and instruction. *Studies in Second Language Acquisition, 21*(1), 81–108.

Munro, M. J. & Derwing, T. M. (1999). Foreign accent, comprehensibility, and intelligibility in the speech of second language learners. *Language Learning, 49*(Suppl. 1), 285–310.

Neeley, T. (2012, May). Global business speaks English. Why you need a language strategy now. *Harvard Business Review*, 116–124.

Roth, W. M. (2002). From action to discourse: The bridging function of gestures. *Cognitive Systems Research, 3*(1–4), 535–554.

Saville-Troike, M. (1985). The place of silence in an integrated theory of communication. In: D. Tannen & M. Saville-Troike (Eds.), *Perspectives on silence* (pp. 3–18). Norwood, NJ: Ablex.

Schneider, E. W. (2007). *Post-colonial English: Varieties around the world*. Cambridge, UK: Cambridge University Press.

Stubbe, M. (1997). Are you listening? Cultural influences on the use of supportive verbal feedback in conversation. *Journal of Pragmatics, 29*, 257–289.

Tiersma, P. (1995). The Language of Silence. *Rutgers Law Review, 48*, 1–99.

Wells, J. C. (1982). *Accents of English 3: Beyond the British Isles*. Cambridge, UK: Cambridge University Press.

Yashima, T. (2002). Willingness to communicate in L2: The Japanese EFL context. *Modern Language Journal, 86*, 54–66.

POST-READING QUESTIONS

1. So far, what has been the most difficult or challenging language you've tried to learn? Why?
2. How do you think your native language "sounds" to people who don't speak it?
3. In your history of studying English, what aspects of the language have you had the most problems with?
4. What language sounds the most beautiful to your own ears?
5. What language do you think you might find most difficult to master? Which other language would you most like to learn?

6. According to the text, what factors have contributed to the dominance of English as the global lingua franca?

7. Restate in your own words the advantages presented in the reading for using English in international business and scientific research.

8. In your own words, summarize the features of English that make it somewhat easier to learn in comparison to other languages mentioned in the text.

VOCABULARY WORK

PART A

From the reading text, find the words or phrases that have similar meanings to the words / phrases given in the numbered lists below. The first one has been done for you as an example.

From Paragraphs A–H:	Synonymous Word or Phrase
1. peers; equivalents in role; coequals; rivals; partners	counterparts (paragraph E)
2. portraying; describing; characterizing	____________
3. something that is easy; easy as pie	____________
4. projects; ventures; operations; enterprises	____________
5. at the forefront; very advanced technologically	____________
6. eliminated; got rid of	____________
7. eliminated; did away with	____________
8. many-sided	____________
9. privilege or right; choice	____________
10. factual	____________
11. to make up; to compose	____________
12. hurdles; hindrances	____________
13. required; binding; mandatory	____________
14. slimmed down in contour or profile; made less bulky	____________

15. intimidating; extremely challenging ____________________
16. gathered; composite; clustered; assembled ____________________
17. of two tongues or languages ____________________
18. bombardment; profusion; plethora ____________________
19. words that sound the same; words that are pronounced the same ____________________
20. in an intimidating manner; arduously ____________________
21. incomprehensible; indecipherable ____________________

From Paragraphs I–T: Synonymous Word or Phrase

22. tormenting; taunting; bedeviling ____________________
23. augmented by; complemented by; strengthened; intensified by ____________________
24. surpass in number ____________________
25. probability ____________________
26. a district or county in New York City ____________________
27. antiquated; obsolete; outdated ____________________
28. two or more vowel sounds spoken together as a gliding sound ____________________
29. fellow countrymen or countrywomen ____________________
30. be adequate; be enough; to fulfill ____________________
31. uncompromising; intransigent; unyielding ____________________
32. of the highest order or rank; predominant; supreme; cardinal ____________________
33. reserved; quiet; taciturn; tight-lipped ____________________
34. behavior; conduct ____________________
35. to overcome the initial reserve between strangers to engage in conversation ____________________
36. rhythmic flow; beat ____________________

37. aspects; sides ____________________

38. be reluctant to do; be averse to do; be disinclined to do ____________________

39. locating exactly; describing precisely ____________________

VOCABULARY WORK

PART B

Choose an appropriate form of one of the words given below to complete the numbered sentences that follow. Two of the words have been used twice.

CONSTITUTE	LIKELY
CUTTING-EDGE	OBLIGE
DAUNT	OBSTACLE
DEPICT	PARAMOUNT
DIE-HARD	PINPOINT
DO AWAY WITH	PREROGATIVE
ENHANCE	UNINTELLIGENT

1. In the United States, the ____________________ of an individual being killed by lightning is 30 times higher than that of being attacked by a shark.

2. Mysterious codes, texts, and scripts—such as Linear A, the Voynich Manuscript, the Indus Script, the Rohonc Codex, Rongorongo, and the Beale Ciphers—remain completely ____________________ to cryptologists even today, despite many attempts to decipher the messages they contain.

3. Ship captains now use sophisticated radar and sonar equipment as early-warning systems for dangerous submarine ____________________ such as icebergs.

4. In most Japanese households, visitors are ____________________ to remove their shoes before entering the host's apartment or house.

5. By and large, computer systems have ____________________ the need for typewriters.

6. The vast majority of photographs created today are ________________ in some way using computer applications dedicated to the sophisticated manipulation of digital images.

7. It has always been the _________________________ of the victors of armed conflicts to interpret and record the history of the circumstances and causes that led to war.

8. Frequent brushing and flossing are of _________________________ importance for the maintenance of good oral hygiene.

9. For many individuals who suffer from depression, it is often difficult to _________________________ any single, specific cause for their melancholy state of mind.

10. Poor computer skills are a major _________________________ for many who are trying to (re-)enter the workforce.

11. Despite hundreds of military and civilian photographs as well as thousands of eyewitness accounts, _________________________ skeptics are still unwilling to entertain the possibility that earth has been visited by UFOs.

12. German manufacturers of optical equipment have a long tradition of producing _________________________ lens designs.

13. Despite his lifelong weak physical _________________________, Immanuel Kant lived to the ripe old age of 80.

14. Many renaissance paintings _________________________ scenes specifically requested by wealthy merchants or noblemen who had commissioned the works from individual artists.

15. Becoming a proficient speaker of any tone language such as Thai, Mandarin, Vietnamese, or Cantonese, is a _________________________ task even for the most talented learners.

16. Picasso's _________________________ of the bombing of the Spanish city of Guernica has become one of the most haunting representations of twentieth-century art.

LANGUAGE FOCUS

PART C

1. In paragraph A, find pronouns used as sentence subjects.

2. Identify instances of grammatical parallelism in paragraph B.

3. In paragraphs B–D, identify present participles used as adjectives. [Note that present participles and gerunds have the same grammatical form but different syntactic functions, e.g., eating, writing, working, walking, etc.]

4. In paragraphs D–F, find adverbs that modify adjectives. Find the passive verb phrases used in paragraphs K–N and identify their tense. [For a review of the PASSIVE VOICE, see the APPENDIX, section F.]

5. In paragraphs K and L, identify the simple subjects in each sentence, i.e., the subject that agrees with the finite sentence verb.

Sentence Transformation

For questions 6–10, use the word given below the first sentence to complete the second sentence in the blanks provided. Use between three and eight words including the given word. The given word must NOT be changed in any way, and the meaning of the sentences should be as similar as possible.

Example: We eagerly await a renewed encounter with you in the future.
forward
We are really <u>looking forward to seeing</u> you again in the future.

6. Many people are simply unfit for stressful jobs.
cut
Many people ______________________________ extremely stressful jobs.

7. Several of us were quite annoyed at Timothy when he refused to help us with the first draft of our proposal.
off
Several of us were quite ______________________________ refusal to help us with the first draft of our proposal.

8. The company CEO went out of his way to make light of the firm's third-quarter loss.

   play

   The company CEO went out of his way ________________________ the firm's third-quarter loss.

9. If you put in one additional hour per day over the next eight days, you can compensate for the day you were absent.

   make

   You ____ the day you were absent if you put in one additional hour per day over the next eight days.

10. Most of the problems the firm is experiencing can be attributed to poor management.

    boil

    Most of the problems the firm is experiencing ____________________ poor management.

PART D

ULTIMATE CHALLENGE

Sentence Reconstruction

Reconstruct the following ten sentences by putting the individual words back into their correct order. All of the sentences represent TRUE statements that can be inferred from the information presented in the reading text. Supply appropriate punctuation as needed.

1. to it in to a in at are are peer when scientists communicate reviewed English published who journals comes disadvantage distinct unable getting

   ____

   ____

   ____

2. speakers speakers of non-native English native outnumber greatly

____

____

____

3. do of not the nouns highly unlike gender languages systems have inflecting nominal English

____

____

____

4. of by in all tones are Mandarin possible one Chinese characterized words four

____

____

____

5. of of on an consonants word complex standard three grammar Arabic roots system extremely consisting based displays

____

____

____

6. has as is a an markings given language evidentiary example that of obligatory Tseze

____

____

____

7. for of and the Western challenging Hindi languages phonological present learners Urdu very problems

____

____

____

8. of of communication an in is cultures successful some essential form many feature feedback

____

____

____

9. a in and the language roles motivation second important play acquisition ability of

____

____

____

10. in the wide even pronunciation there within country variations English often same regional are speaking

____

____

____

PART E

LANGUAGE IN USE

I Suggested Questions for Discussion

A. Describe some of the key lexical / grammatical features of your native language.

B. What features of your native language are especially difficult for non-native speakers to learn and master?

C. Which words or phrases in your native language do you believe are impossible to translate into English?

II Suggested Questions for Written Research Projects

A. After conducting appropriate background research, write a brief history of your native language that includes its origin and subsequent development.

B. Write a description of key lexical / grammatical features of your native language as if you were writing a Wikipedia entry. You may also include elements of A (first writing task) in your description.

C. Describe and outline your own topic-related research question.

SOCIAL NETWORKS AND THE REVOLUTION IN COMMUNICATION

UNIT 5

BEFORE YOU READ

What are the advantages of being a member of social media platforms such as Facebook? What disadvantages might be involved?

DIRECTIONS: As you read the following text, fill in the numbered blanks with ONE suitable word.

CLOZE TASK

A Very few developments in the modern era have had as profound an effect on the [1]____________________ we live, work, play, plan, and interact as the Internet. From its relatively humble commercial beginnings in the 1990s, the Internet has grown into a social, political, financial, and technological behemoth that has become vital to civilization as we [2]____________________ it.

B Within this remarkable achievement spectrum, social networks and social media enjoy a special status [3]____________________ for no other reason than the mind-boggling numbers of people who are interconnected through them. Facebook, which made its cyber-debut in 2004, rocketed into second position just behind Google in terms of total numbers of users, boasting no fewer than 670 million at the beginning of 2011. In May of 2012, Facebook was traded for the first time on Wall Street as a public firm, with an initial offering value estimated at $38 per share, and a user base in excess of 900 million.

C When in the early months of 2011 an ever-increasing number of citizens in Tunisia, Egypt, Algeria, Libya, Yemen, Bahrain, Morocco, and Syria took to the streets of their capitals to demonstrate for a greater participatory role of civil society in shaping policies in those countries, the outside world followed much of the turmoil via Facebook, Twitter, and YouTube. Cell phones equipped with cameras of even moderate resolution allow ordinary citizens to record events as they [4]________________, and within minutes upload the footage or images onto appropriate social networking sites—from where they then often "go viral." Within hours, the entire world becomes aware of newsworthy [5]____________________ and history in the making. Today, citizens in strife-torn areas are actively encouraged to carry their cell phones with them at all [6]______________, just in case circumstances warrant worldwide attention to events as they develop. Through specialized apps, users can upload photos, video clips, texts, documents, and voice messages to [7]____________________ with the entire world.

Image production credit: iStock.com/londoneye

D Social networking sites are also valuable [8]____________________ for corporations. As a very low-cost but effective channel for marketing products, small click-on display ads can dramatically increase a company's exposure and greatly expand its base of potential [9]__________________. Such sites are also excellent public relations forums, allowing clever strategists to correct unwanted negative perceptions of the [10]______________ image. At the same time, marketing specialists can learn a great deal about the public's preferences for competing products and the reasons one specific brand is hot, while another is not.

E The field of education has also benefited from the proliferation of the extensive array of networking opportunities. Parents and teachers can easily exchange important information about a child's learning progress and address particular [11]_________________ either party might have. Teachers can post new assignments, update curricula, and schedule online chat room sessions.

F The highly innovative features of networking sites have also permeated essentially every aspect of the healthcare [12]_____________. One important niche to emerge from the now ubiquitous platform has been the focused support group for patients and clients with any number of physical, mental, or emotional problems. Sites such as Caring Bridge and PatientsLikeMe offer family and friends the [13]_________________ to stay constantly informed about a loved one's medical condition, follow-up treatments, and progress through rehabilitation. Those seeking help with substance abuse or other forms of addiction can also find many different support forums, such as SoberCircle and DailyStrength, with vast numbers of members scattered all around the world. Studies have shown that individuals who are actively [14]_________________ in social networks specifically devoted to people suffering from similar health-related problems enjoy much higher success rates in overcoming addiction, as well as faster recuperation times after serious injury or illness (Eysenbach, 2003; Fox & Fallows, 2003; Horrigan, 2001; Preece, 2000).

G But this interconnected world is not without its dark [15]_______. Sociologists and communication specialists have not even begun to grasp the long-term implications of all that the universal visibility of our most private thoughts, feelings, wants, and anxieties brings with it (Joinson, 1998). Allowing our fingers to fire off our innermost desires and fears in the intimacy of our own four walls on our very own keypad is deceptively easy and innocent. What appears to be harmlessly private, [16]___________ only for the chosen "friends" we [17]_________________ into our inner cyber-sanctorum, is potentially "out there" for the whole world to read and analyze, for as long as digital data collections may exist.

H A growing number of corporations have started using data mining applications to weed out undesirable job [18]__________________. And just what might fall under the category of "undesirable"? It may include people whose public persona—on display in its best behavior during the interview—conflicts with their thousands of Facebook comments; or whose impeccably polished business attire is clearly missing in the (semi-)nude racy image posted for the community of friends to see. According to a report in the August 20, 2009, [19]__________________ of the *New York Times* entitled "More Employers Use Social Networks to Check Out Applicants," over 50% of the employers who were interviewed admitted that provocative or sexually explicit photos on social networking sites were the primary reason that candidates for jobs did not get [20]____________.

I Of perhaps even greater concern is the potential for identity theft, the fastest-growing type of crime associated with Internet-based data. Resourceful criminals exploit casual comments and details about a group member's [21]__________________ background to build up an entire profile of their unsuspecting victim—date and place of birth, mother's maiden name, father's occupation—each time adding just a little bit more to the personal dossier.

J Particularly disheartening and worrisome is a trend that has become too commonplace in Japan, especially among young people. Teenage years are often the most difficult period in any person's life, irrespective of cultural background. When young people become isolated from others or experience bullying at school, various types of depression may [22] ________________ in with dire consequences. The Internet and various social networking sites have become the most common forum in Japan for what has become known as "suicide pacts" (Lewis, 2004). Groups of young people collectively arrange for a group suicide, with most of the details concerning time, place, and methods worked out in advance. Clearly, this disturbing phenomenon signals an urgent [23]__________________ for parents, teachers, and counselors to be increasingly alert to possible signs of depression among school-age children [24]__________________ that appropriate intervention regimens might be implemented. It should be hoped that the Internet and social networking sites might provide a forum for mutual support and mental healing, just as they have done for people afflicted with various physical illnesses and substance-abuse problems.

K Despite all its existing and potential drawbacks, the communications revolution has even managed to change the English language itself. As is so often the case with new products and processes that quickly establish [25]____________________ in the population as given standards, "Twitter" (the name of both the company and the social network the company created) may be used as a regular English verb: infinitive—to Twitter (notice the capital letter); past tense—Twittered; past participle—Twittered. The derived form "tweet" also has similar grammatical forms and functions: noun—a tweet; infinitive—to tweet; past tense—tweeted; past participle—tweeted. Now, how about "Facebook" as a verb?

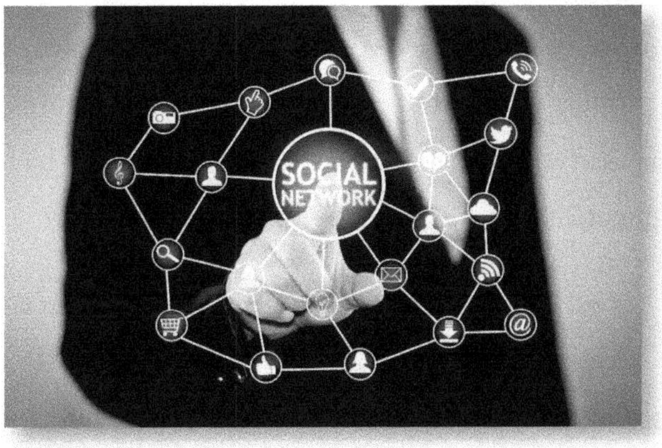

Image production credit: iStock.com/hh5800

L Facebook founder Mark Zuckerberg was once asked via instant message how the company was able to coax out the most private information from its members. His response, which was first reported by Nicholas Carlson at the *Silicon Valley Insider* and later confirmed by Jose Antonio Vargas in *The New Yorker* was simple: "They 'trust me'. Dumb f****."

M Despite his still relatively young age, Zuckerberg proved to be a very savvy businessman. Trading involving Facebook's initial IPO in May of 2012 turned [26]____________________ to be nothing short of a complete disaster for investors, with accusations of "insider trading" and "pump and dump" maneuvers surfacing from all corners of the business community. It appears that a number of "better informed" investors including Zuckerberg himself knew that something was not quite kosher with the money-making scheme behind the company, which may explain why he sold 30.2 million shares of his own stock at $37.58 per share, before the value plummeted hours later. Hundreds of lawsuits [27]____________ against a number of brokerage houses and against Zuckerberg himself may well have the last word in such questionable business practices, which, according to Elizabeth Ody and Margaret Collins of *Bloomberg News*, were seen as "deepening investor distrust of stocks."

N Concerns about Facebook's exponential rise were not limited to Wall Street equities markets. A growing trend among companies seeking to hire new staff is to insist that prospective candidates for a given position "friend" members of the hiring committee. By gaining access to the job applicant's Facebook pages, companies claim that they're better able to [28]____________________ the "real" person behind the application. Applicants who refuse to grant the company access to their Facebook accounts are simply eliminated from the pool. Several US-based tech-oriented companies whose central focus is social media have reported that their entire applications process is done on Facebook.

O These types of practices raise immediate concerns about users' privacy rights. As reported by Harriet Alexander (2014) in *The Sunday Telegraph*, Facebook had engaged in a research experiment on 689,003 of its users in January of 2012, without ever disclosing to the users that they were being used as unwitting guinea pigs.

P Published in the *Proceedings of the National Academy of Sciences* (June 17, 2014), the study showed quite convincingly that users tend to react positively to favorable posts by posting positive messages of their own. Conversely, negative or unfavorable postings tend to elicit negative postings from friends who read them. Since Facebook uses elaborate algorithms to select which newsfeeds to show which users, it's easy to see how users could be directed into thinking or feeling a certain way.

Q Critique of Facebook's experimental procedures, in particular of its failure to disclose to users that they were being manipulated and used, was swift and massive. "Just what else might they be doing with us that they aren't telling us about?" many users wondered. PNAS itself took the extraordinary step of publishing an "Editorial Expression of Concern," penned by the editor-in-chief of the publication, Inder M. Verma (2014). While acknowledging the valuable contribution of the Facebook study in an "important and emerging area of social science research," the editor expressed concern that neither the authors of the study nor Facebook itself had asked for or received permission from the participants in the research project. However, the "common rule" requiring informed consent from test subjects is a legal issue, the editor noted, and "as a private company Facebook was under no obligation to conform to the provisions of the Common Rule when it collected the data used by the authors, and the Common Rule does not preclude their use of the data."

R Despite the criticism directed at social media and their suspected participation in surveillance schemes to track and monitor ordinary citizens, it would seem that the phenomenon at large is here to stay. Different versions or take-offs of Facebook have also become popular in other parts of the world. China's (人人网) Ren Ren Wang ("everybody's website"), which debuted in 2005, had logged more than 200 million users by 2013. Likewise, VKontakte has become the second largest social network after Facebook, catering primarily to Russian-language users in Eastern Europe and Central Asia. Started in 2006, VK.com already had close to 240 million participants registered by 2014.

S In all their sundry forms, social media have truly transformed the way humans connect and communicate. They have moved us much closer to a single global community in which each participant, in theory, can follow anyone else's life story as it [29]____________________. One has to wonder, though, if this is always a good thing. Have we inadvertently transformed ourselves into Orwellian subjects?

T Social networks provide a valuable tool for people of all ages to [30]____________________ out to one another in ways never imagined by previous generations. Their enormous potential for growth is matched by their equally valuable contributions to the health, education, and welfare of people all around the world, [31]__________________ us to grow together in a community of global interests for the betterment of the entire planet.

REFERENCES

Alexander, H. (2014, June 29). Facebook conducted secret psychology experiment on users' emotions. *The Telegraph.* Retrieved November 9, 2014, from http://www.telegraph.co.uk/technology/facebook/10932534/Facebook-conducted-secret-psychology-experiment-on-users-emotions.html

Eysenbach, G. (2003). The impact of the Internet on cancer outcomes. CA: *A Cancer Journal for Clinicians, 53,* 356–371.

Fox, S. & Fallows, D. (2003). Internet health resources. Washington, D.C. Pew Internet & American Life Project.

Horrigan, J. (2001). Online communities: Networks that nurture long-distance relationships and local ties. Washington, D.C. Pew Internet & American Life Project.

Joinson, A. (1998). Causes and Implications of Disinhibited Behavior on the Internet. In: J. Gackenbach (Ed.). (2006). *Psychology and the Internet. Intrapersonal, Interpersonal, and Transpersonal Implications* (pp. 43–60). New York: Academic Press.

Lewis, L. (2004, October 13). Internet suicide pacts shock Japan. *The Times,* p. 15.

Preece, J. (2000). *Online communities: Designing usability, supporting sociability.* Chichester, UK: John Wiley & Sons Ltd.

Verma, I. (2014) Editorial expression of Concern: Experimental evidence of massivescale emotional contagion through social networks. *PNAS 2014 111* (29) 10779; published ahead of print July 3, 2014, doi:10.1073/pnas.1412469111

POST-READING QUESTIONS

1. What (if any) of the information presented in the reading was new to you?
2. What information (if any) did you find of interest?
3. Have you ever posted anything on a social media site that you later regretted?
4. From your own personal experience, what is the most annoying thing about social media?
5. What aspects (if any) of the Internet do you feel should be government-controlled?

6. Describe the role of social media in recent political movements.
7. In your own words, summarize the ways in which patients can benefit from social media.
8. What is the "dark side" of social media? What dangers do these new forms of communication pose for individual privacy and security?

VOCABULARY WORK

PART A

From the reading text, find the words or phrases that have similar meanings to the words / phrases given in the numbered lists below. The first one has been done for you as an example.

From Paragraphs A–G:	Synonymous Word or Phrase
1. scenes or reels from a motion picture	footage (paragraph C)
2. restoration; renewal; reparation; mending; amelioration	____________
3. mentally, psychologically, or emotionally overwhelming	____________
4. privacy; closeness to another in a private manner	____________
5. penetrated; passed into; filtered into	____________
6. pathway; approach; route	____________
7. an entity of gigantic size	____________
8. soared; climbed; shot up	____________
9. defeating; besting; surmounting	____________
10. holding; possessing; sporting; flaunting	____________
11. disseminated; spread out	____________
12. misleadingly; illusively	____________
13. gained an advantage from; profited from	____________
14. violence; rebellion; uprising; uproar	____________
15. popular; in demand	____________

16. deserve; justify; call for ______________

17. poignant; acute; intense; deep in meaning ______________

18. premiere; initial appearance; launch; beginning ______________

From Paragraphs H–T: Synonymous Word or Phrase

19. offhand; offhanded; cursory; loose; informal ______________

20. shrewdly informed or aware of; canny ______________

21. saddening; distressing ______________

22. to screen or filter out ______________

23. spotlessly; perfectly; flawlessly ______________

24. tempting; beguiling; inciting; exciting; stimulating ______________

25. through; by means of ______________

26. pure and acceptable for consumption by Jews; legitimate ______________

27. unaware; off guard; trusting; credulous ______________

28. finished; refined; cultured; genteel; perfected ______________

29. elicit; bring out; draw out ______________

30. emerging; appearing ______________

31. clothes; dress; apparel ______________

32. nose-dived ______________

33. in dispute; debatable; moot; open to doubt; controversial ______________

34. a collection of files or documents pertaining to a topic or person ______________

35. sexually enticing or provocative ______________

36. improvement ____________________

37. usual; ordinary; mundane; general; run-of-the-mill ____________________

PART B

VOCABULARY WORK

Choose an appropriate form of one of the words given below to complete the numbered sentences that follow. Two of the words have been used twice.

BENEFIT	POLISH
CASUAL	PROFOUND
COMMONPLACE	PROVOKE
DEBUT	QUESTION
FOOT	SAVVY
OVERCOME	SURFACE
PLUMMET	WARRANT

1. The now-retired American spy plane, SR 71—also known as "Black Bird"—made its service ________________________ in 1964.

2. Garlic, turmeric, pumpkin, ginger, and fish oil have been shown to be very ________________________ to patients suffering from various forms of chronic inflammation.

3. The "Zapruder film," which is ________________________ taken of the actual assassination of U.S. President John F. Kennedy as the killing unfolded, has become one of the most renowned pieces of documentary film ever recorded.

4. Frankly, in our view, the negative ad hominem attacks our opponent has launched in his candidacy do not even ________________________ a response.

5. Franz Kafka's novels and short stories portray deeply thought-________________________ motifs and plots in which individuals become trapped in impossible circumstances and arcane bureaucratic labyrinths.

BENEFIT	POLISH
CASUAL	PROFOUND
COMMONPLACE	PROVOKE
DEBUT	QUESTION
FOOT	SAVVY
OVERCOME	SURFACE
PLUMMET	WARRANT

6. Upon the death of North Korean leader Kim Jung Il, television broadcasts showed thousands of North Korean citizens completely ________________________ with emotion.

7. News of the collapse of New York investment giant Lehman Brothers sent stock markets ________________________ worldwide, with the Dow Jones index shaving off more than 770 points in a single day.

8. With its vast resources of tools and information covering essentially the entire spectrum of human knowledge, the Internet has ________________ affected the way we live, work, play, date, and otherwise relate to our entire planet.

9. Job applicants are always advised to ________________________ their CVs and resumes before sending out application packages.

10. Unfortunately, those conducting the interview felt that Paul was simply too ________________________ dressed for the occasion; in fact, he was reportedly even wearing a T-shirt.

11. One of the most famous Latin expressions still used today reads: cui bono?—or in English: who ________________________, or who stands to gain?

12. I was astonished that the director was offended by what I thought was nothing more than a ________________________ comment about the weather.

13. The use of cell phones and their many applications is so ____________ today that many people don't know how they would survive without them.

14. News of the tragedy didn't ______________________ until the responsible agencies had double-checked all the facts, and even then the spokespersons were anything but forthcoming with details.

15. ______________________ tax accountants can exploit every possible loophole in the existing tax laws to save their clients as much money as is legally possible.

16. The use of capital punishment as a crime deterrent is highly ______________________ and does not appear to be supported by factual evidence.

PART C

LANGUAGE FOCUS

1. Identify the complete sentence subjects in each sentence in paragraphs B and C.

2. Identify instances of sentence inversion in paragraphs I and J. [For a review of sentence INVERSION, see the APPENDIX, section E.]

3. Find the passive verb phrases used in paragraphs K–M and identify their tense. [For a review of the PASSIVE VOICE, see the APPENDIX, section F.]

4. What antecedent noun does the pronoun "its" refer to in the phrase ". . . on display in its best behavior" (paragraph H)?

5. What would be a synonymous expression for "strife-torn areas" in paragraph C?

Sentence Transformation

For questions 6–10, use the word given below the first sentence to complete the second sentence in the blanks provided. Use between three and eight words including the given word. The given word must NOT be changed in any way, and the meaning of the sentences should be as similar as possible.

Example: We eagerly await a renewed encounter with you in the future.

forward

We are really <u>looking forward to seeing</u> you again in the future.

6. This performance setback is attributable to the team's lack of preparation and practice.

   chalked

   The team's poor performance can ____________________ a lack of preparation and practice.

7. The new tax laws have largely eliminated government audits.

   done

   The new tax laws have largely ____________________ government audits.

8. David is simply not capable of leading this team.

   task

   David is simply not ____________________ leading this team.

9. At this rate, it's impossible to predict how long construction of the new wing will take.

   telling

   At this rate, there's ____________________ construction of the new wing will take.

10. The board of directors insist that they were absolutely clueless that a hostile takeover was being attempted.

    whatsoever

    The board of directors insist that they had ____________________ that a hostile takeover was being attempted.

ULTIMATE CHALLENGE

PART D

Sentence Reconstruction

Reconstruct the following ten sentences by putting the individual words back into their correct order. All of the sentences represent TRUE statements that can be inferred from the information presented in the reading text. Supply appropriate punctuation as needed.

1. of of the throughout connect people sites millions media world

hundreds social

____

____

____

2. in of the policies civil have public role sites shaping participatory networking society increased social

____

____

____

3. in of are can who online find a forums from immediate people support range dedicated afflictions suffering wide

____

____

____

4. a of to of the as is be is what what clear media and appear between our result boundaries social cut public private integration vanishing into lives daily

____

____

____

5. on to use networking applicants mining many sites entries software companies social screen sophisticated data job

____

____

____

6. forums their lured of of details are members providing identity online

about often victims personal into theft history key to

____

____

____

7. on by the of the of networking provided have social feedback aware sites customers importance become increasingly companies

____

____

____

8. on of of the the the time families condition real are patient able updates ill critically provide to

____

____

____

9. on and to or are their their progress time family media from friends often who with illness use updates social recuperating injury patients provide real

____

____

____

10. the the of by sites widespread has networking affected language social been English popularity itself

____

____

____

PART E

LANGUAGE IN USE

I Suggested Questions for Discussion

A. Describe your overall experience of being involved in social networks. What have you gained from this experience? What have been the disadvantages (if any)? What arguments would you use to convince someone of the merits who has thus far been averse to using social networks?

B. Where do you personally draw the line between the public "you" that you choose to present in social media, and the secret, private "you" that you would prefer to keep hidden?

C. Would you willingly allow your parents or your spouse to read all of your postings on your own social media account?

II Suggested Questions for Written Research Projects

A. Noting specific instances, describe the impact social media have had on society in your own country. Assess this impact in relation to the overall levels of civic participation and personal interaction among citizens.

B. How have social media contributed to improvements in education, medical care, entertainment, or political awareness and involvement in your country?

C. Describe and outline your own topic-related research question.

UNIT 6

MONEY MAKES THE WORLD GO ROUND

BEFORE YOU READ

In your view, how true is the old saw that "Money cannot buy happiness"? If money cannot buy happiness, why do so many people around the world strive to become rich?

DIRECTIONS: As you read the following text, complete the blanks after the numbered brackets with an appropriate form of the word given in capital letters. The first one has been done for you as an example.

CLOZE TASK

A Money and wealth represent centerpieces of many [0] LIFE <u>lives</u>, and the love of money has even been called "the root of all evil." When it comes right down to it, most people around the world, [1] RESPECT ____________________ of the culture they've grown up in, long to be well-off, to have enough money to be able to afford anything their hearts might long for. Many of us envy the glamorous lifestyles of the rich and famous, the jet-setters who can fly off to their own private island at a moment's notice, without having to answer to anyone.

B The term "millionaire" used to be the golden standard by which [2] MONEY____________________ success was judged; today, it's "billionaire." For many years, the moniker "richest person on the planet" was held by computer whiz and Harvard dropout, Bill Gates, founder of Microsoft. But times have changed, and so has the location of wealth and assets; [3]

GLOBE_____________________ has effected massive shifts in wealth and poverty patterns. According to Forbes.com, as of 2011 the United States still had the highest number of billionaires in [4] PERCENT___________ terms (40%), but its grip on these positions has been slipping, with both China and Russia logging in big gains in the total number of billionaires worldwide. According to a Bloomberg (de Jong, 2012) report, eight out of ten of the world's [5] WEALTH__________________ countries are in Asia (Switzerland—in the fourth position—and the United States were the [6] EXCEPT__________________ to the rule). Singapore occupied the top spot on the list, with Qatar and Kuwait coming in in second and third positions, respectively. Hong Kong was listed in position number five, with the United Arab Emirates, the United States, Israel, Taiwan, and Bahrain rounding out the top ten in that order.

Image production credit: iStock.com/vkyryl

Image production credit: iStock.com/imaginima

C Although most people recognize the presence of "big money" when they see it, far fewer actually know where money comes from, and this is especially true in the case of Americans and the U.S. dollar. When asked point blank, "Where does money come from?", most people tend to respond with some [7] VARY__________________ of "the government prints it." But that is not really true at all.

D According to the information pamphlet entitled "Modern Money Mechanics," originally published by the Public Information Center of the Federal Reserve Bank of Chicago in 1961, the process works like this: When the U.S. government needs money, it issues bonds or treasury notes in certain denominations. These are essentially nothing but IOUs, or promises to pay the debt sum designated by the denomination on the bill or bond, plus interest. Traditionally, U.S. government debt has been considered the safest possible investment because these IOUs or bonds carry the full credibility of the U.S. American government itself and its promise to pay. The Federal Reserve gives the government in exchange for these treasury IOUs a "teletronic"—or Federal Reserve check—which is backed by absolutely nothing. The U.S. government then "deposits" this check into its account with one of the Federal Reserve regional banks. The bank enters the sum once as a [8] LIABLE____________________ (since the entry is accredited to the government's account), and once as an asset (because the bank can use the deposit to issue loans). In reality, all that this procedure involves is a few entries into the "Fedwire" computer transfer network.

Image production credit: iStock.com/skyhobo

Image production credit: iStock.com/Jitalia17

E From the government's account, millions of [9] RECEIVE ____________________ are paid with checks that are then signed by the U.S. government on the holdings [10] ELECTRONIC________________ credited to its account through the Federal Reserve purchase of the government's debt. It is through these deposits that the vast bulk of the money supply is generated. The recipients then deposit these government checks into their own personal or company bank account.

F This all seems fairly straightforward, until on closer inspection we discover the astonishing trick involved. If, for example, the government sells debt (bonds) in the amount of $10 billion and the government account is credited with that same amount in the Federal Reserve's banking system, the banks themselves are then allowed to lend out, with interest, $9 billion on top of the original deposit, which the bank creates out of nothing. The recipient(s) of a loan for the amount of this newly created $9 billion would

[11] PRESUME____________________ in turn deposit this money into their own banking accounts. The banks again retain 10% of this amount as their "minimum reserve requirement" and lend out—again with interest—the newly created sum of $8.1 billion. This sum is then deposited into an account, the bank retains 10% of that ($810 million) as its minimum reserve requirement, and creates out of thin air an [12] ADD____________ $7.29 billion, which it in turn lends out with interest. The $7.29 billion is then deposited into the account of someone else, the bank keeps 10% of that ($729 million) on hold as its minimum reserve, and creates another $6.561 billion, which it disperses further, with interest. This process is repeated over and over, and each time the bank magically creates nine times the amount of every given deposit. Thanks to the money multiplier, a purchase of assets of $10 billion by the Federal Reserve, which it pays for with nothing but a computer entry, generates "very quickly a tenfold" $100 billion "increase in the money supply of the banking system as a whole."

G It becomes readily apparent that, based on the mechanics of this money-making scheme, it is never in the best interest of the banks for customers or clients to pay off their loans. A homebuyer who obtains a fixed-rate mortgage at 7% for a 22.5-year period on a loan of $95,000 would end up paying $93,780 in interest alone, thus nearly doubling the total cost of the house. If the [13] BORROW____________________ surprisingly paid off the entire amount within two months, the bank would naturally lose the enormous sums of interest it would otherwise accrue. When entire countries are the recipients of loans, banks earn tens or hundreds of billions in interest [14] PAY____________________ over time.

H One puzzling question remains: since technically only the principal is being created through the mechanics of this debt-based monetary system, how is the money created to pay off the interest charged by the banks each step of the way? The answer of course is that it isn't! This elaborate type of Ponzi scheme has been compared to the children's game "musical chairs": when the music stops, someone is left out in the cold.

I Soberly assessing the money creation process back in his day, Henry Ford, [15] FOUND_____________________ of the Ford Motor Corporation, once had this to say: "It is well that the people of the nation do not understand our banking and monetary system, for if they did, I believe there would be a revolution before tomorrow morning."

J These insights explain in part why a grassroots [16] MOVE __________________ in the USA has been gaining ground to create a banking system that reflects the needs of the public itself as opposed to the wants of bankers. The Public Banking Institute believes that the country as a whole will be much better off, if and when all the interest earned on debt is reinvested in public institutions and infrastructure.

K The debt accrued through massive trade deficits has crippled many communities in the USA. Even in terms of the benefits that the U.S. was allegedly going to reap through globalization, the outcome has been dismal. The [17] INDUSTRY_____________________ base of the country has been decimated, and according to Pisano and Shih (2009), the United States is no longer even able to manufacture a Kindle. Thousands of companies across the land had followed the advice of Wall Street to outsource many of the low-value-added tasks involved in manufacturing to cheap-labor countries like China, and to use the savings to concentrate on innovation, research, and development. In assessing the overall impact that outsourcing as one aspect of globalization has had on U.S. industry, Pisano and Shih conclude that in reality, "the U.S. has lost or is in the process of losing the knowledge, skilled people, and [18] SUPPLY_______________ infrastructure needed to manufacture many of the cutting-edge products it invented" (p. 116).

L According to McMillion (as cited in Buchanan, 2012, pp. 15–16), with a net loss of more than three million jobs between December 2000 and December 2010, the United States experienced the worst decline in industrial production and private sector employment since the decade that began in 1928. In the same time frame, total trade deficits exceeded $6 trillion, with $2 trillion of that sum recorded with China alone. For many years, the United States also [19] BODY____________________ the pinnacle of high-tech industrial production and export, but from 2007 through 2010, the U.S. trade deficit with China for advanced technological products amounted to more than $300 billion. By 2008, more than 70% of U.S. gross domestic product was the result of consumer spending on goods and services (Moore, 2011). Neither individuals nor companies nor nations can continuously spend more than they earn, and current account deficits of this magnitude are [20] SUSTAIN____________________, as they have required the U.S. to borrow from abroad to the tune of $1.5 billion on a daily basis.

M As it stands now, many [21] ECONOMY____________________ predict that deeply [22] DEBT____________________ countries such as the United States will never be in the position to repay the trillions of dollars they owe. The money needed to cover just the interest rates alone cuts [23] HEAVY____________________ into the country's total income. Many leading financial experts and investment gurus have warned of the long-term consequences of continually high trade deficits and budget gaps (Buffett & Loomis, 2003; Dickson, 2009). To make matters even worse for the U.S. dollar, the BRICS nations (Brazil, Russia, India, China, and South Africa) announced in July of 2014 that they would collectively pursue an alternative global currency exchange system independent of the U.S. monetary framework. The fear among many economists immediately arose that this would eventually lead to the repatriation of vast sums of U.S. dollars, with inflation then spiraling out of control as a result.

N In Europe, the national debt levels of the Mediterranean rim countries also reached [24] CALAMITY____________________ levels as was evident in the [25] TUMULT____________________ events in Greece during much of 2011 and 2012. The debt to GDP ratios in Italy, Spain, Portugal, and Ireland had also reached intolerable levels during the same period. In Spain, this led to several bank runs in which citizens [26] DRAW____________________ as much money as possible from the banks out of sheer fear that these might become completely [27] SOLVE____________________ and would hence be forced to shut their doors. Urgent European Union-wide talks were set in motion to shore up the failing banks and to provide the needed [28] LIQUID______________ to allow businesses and industry to obtain credit. But the outlook was equally dire for Japan, where the debt to GDP had already reached the 200% level by the end of 2011.

O Perhaps one day the debts of these countries will be forgiven; perhaps one day the billions that would otherwise be spent to cover the interest rates will be used to invest in the people and a much-needed renewal of infrastructure. Today, those prospects are mere pipe dreams.

P Debts as far as the eye can see will [29] NECESSARY ___________ fundamental changes in many countries of the [30] INDUSTRY __________________ world. And the brunt of the impact these changes will have on societies will most likely be carried, as always, by the most vulnerable.

REFERENCES

Buchanan, P. (2012). *Suicide of a superpower. Will America survive to 2025?* New York, NY: Thomas Dunne Books.

Buffett, W. & Loomis, C. (2003, November 10). America's growing trade deficit is selling the nation out from under us. Here's a way to fix the problem and we need to do it now. *Fortune*. Retrieved December 15, 2014 from http://archive.fortune.com/magazines/fortune/fortune_archive/2003/11/10/352872/index.htm

De Jong, D. (2012, May 31). Where the world's millionaires live. *Bloomberg*. Retrieved July 26, 2014 from http://www.bloomberg.com/money-gallery/2012-05-31/where-the-world-s-millionaires-live.html

Dickson, D. M. (2009, February 5). Volcker blames recession on trade imbalances. *Washington Times*.

Moore, S. (2011, April 1). We've become a nation of takers, not makers. *Wall Street Journal*.

Pisano, G. & Shih, W. (2009, July-August). Restoring American competitiveness. *Harvard Business Review*, *87*(7/8), 114–125.

POST-READING QUESTIONS

1. What was the most important piece of information you learned from reading this text?
2. Was there any aspect of the reading that surprised you?
3. According to the reading, what would be the positive benefits of a "public banking" system?
4. How would you explain the "fractional reserve lending" system in your own words?
5. How would you explain what "treasuries" or "government bonds" are?
6. Describe the negative impact of globalization on the US economy, as explained in the text.
7. Explain the meaning of "trade deficits."
8. In your own words, explain the mechanism of money creation in the US Federal Reserve banking system.

VOCABULARY WORK

PART A

From the reading text, find the words or phrases that have similar meanings to the words / phrases given in the numbered lists below. The first one has been done for you as an example.

From Paragraphs A–H:	Synonymous Word or Phrase
1. direct; on target; exactly on a topic	point blank (paragraph C)
2. simple; open; aboveboard; up front; no-nonsense; plain	______________
3. amass; collect; accumulate	______________
4. satisfy debts; settle a debt in full	______________
5. indigence; destitution	______________
6. completing as a final element or item in a list	______________
7. circulates; spreads; disseminates	______________

8. greater part; lion's share ____________
9. believability; reliability; trustworthiness ____________
10. in an instant and without preparation ____________
11. dropping off; waning; declining ____________
12. booking; recording; earning ____________
13. entering a position; crossing a threshold or mark ____________
14. being last in a hopeless position ____________

From Paragraphs I–P:	Synonymous Word or Phrase

15. earn; gain; procure; acquire; come into ____________
16. the basic level; the primary part ____________
17. destroyed to a great extent ____________
18. size; measure; degree; extent ____________
19. novelty; creating new things or methods ____________
20. monetary shortfalls ____________
21. consequence; effect; influence ____________
22. peak; summit; acme; zenith ____________
23. advisors; leaders in a particular field; mentors ____________
24. the fundamental framework of a community, area, or country, including utilities, transportation, etc. ____________
25. debilitated; weakened; impaired ____________
26. full force or impact; effects; consequences ____________
27. fantasy; illusion ____________
28. to support; to buttress; to prop up ____________
29. horrible; awful; dreadful; alarming; grim ____________

VOCABULARY WORK

PART B

Choose an appropriate form of one of the words given below to complete the numbered sentences that follow. Two of the words have been used twice.

ACCRUE	INFRASTRUCTURE
AT A MOMENT'S NOTICE	INNOVATE
BRUNT	PAY OFF
CREDIBLE	PINNACLE
DEFICIT	POVERTY
DIRE	REAP
IMPACT	STRAIGHTFORWARD

1. Because of an 18% rise in imports from OPEC countries and a 22% increase in imports of consumer goods from the Far East, the U.S. current account ________________________ has now reached unsustainable levels.

2. With government deficits running at record-high levels in almost all Western countries, the socioeconomic outlook for many fixed-income retirees is indeed ________________________, and fears are mounting that vast numbers of senior citizens will simply be unable to live on their own in the future or to receive the proper medical care they will require.

3. Communities and states that have found themselves deep in debt have simply been unable to afford major ________________________ projects such as repaving crumbling roads, replacing sagging, corroded bridges, or bolstering giant above-ground parking facilities.

4. Truth be told, banks simply do not want debtors to ________________ their loans in the shortest time possible because that would prevent the lenders from earning the compound interest they would otherwise receive.

5. Criticized by many economists as unacceptably low, the official ________________________ rate in the United States as of 2012 is defined as a four-person-household annual income of $23,050.

6. People from low-context cultures tend to have a very frank, often uncomfortably ________________________ style of communicating.

7. Estimates predict that the ____________________ of a one-mile-wide asteroid with the Pacific Ocean would send a 500-meter wall of water racing eastward as far as Dallas, Texas, destroying virtually everything in its path; the effect would be nearly identical for all nations bordering the western rim of the ocean.

8. Visual displays have benefited tremendously from ________________ designs using organic light-emitting diodes.

9. Tennis legend Steffi Graf reached the ______________________ of her career with her 1999 victory over young Martina Hingis at the French Open tournament in Paris.

10. In many societies around the world, women still do not __________ the same monetary rewards as their male counterparts for an equal or greater quantity of work.

11. Patterns of emigration feature similarities across continents and ages, with persecuted, ______________________ masses seeking a more humane and financially stable life in greener pastures abroad.

12. As ______________________ as it may seem, the two young girls were able to contort their bodies into a clear acrylic box of only nine cubic feet.

13. Having now been shown to have lied on at least three occasions during his testimony, the prosecution's star witness has lost all _______________ in our view.

14. The ______________________ force of the iceberg impact tore a gaping hole into the starboard bow of the Titanic.

15. Your balance of principal plus ______________________ interest stands at $275,000.00.

16. Residents in the coastal regions of Indonesia, the Philippines, Taiwan, and Japan, must be ready ______________________ to move to higher ground following an earthquake.

PART C

LANGUAGE FOCUS

1. Identify all FIRST CONDITIONALS in paragraphs A–I. [For a review of CONDITIONALS, see the APPENDIX, section G.]

2. Identify all ZERO CONDITIONALS in paragraphs A–I.

3. Identify all SECOND CONDITIONALS in paragraphs A–I.

4. Find instances of noun apposition in paragraphs A and B. [An example of apposition: *Khalid, a student from Baghdad, arrived in Sydney on July 10.*]

5. What antecedent noun does the pronoun "it" refer to in the phrase "The answer of course is that it isn't!" in paragraph H?

Sentence Transformation

For questions 6–10, use the word given below the first sentence to complete the second sentence in the blanks provided. Use between three and eight words including the given word. The given word must NOT be changed in any way, and the meaning of the sentences should be as similar as possible.

Example: We eagerly await a renewed encounter with you in the future.
forward
We are really looking forward to seeing you again in the future.

6. News of the coup attempt quickly went viral.
wildfire
News of the coup attempt ____________________.

7. Despite my mother's ripe old age of 97, she stays informed of all the latest news.
abreast
Despite my mother's ripe old age of 97, she ____________________ all the latest news.

8. Luckily, we had developed the delegation's itinerary well ahead of time.
worked
Luckily, we had ____________________ well ahead of time.

9. I'm happy to say that both our children passed their medical license exams with highest marks.

   colors

   I'm happy to say that both our children passed their medical license exams _______________________________________.

10. We managed to install the new operating system with no problem at all.

    hitch

    We managed to install the new operating system ____________________ ____________________.

ULTIMATE CHALLENGE

PART D

Sentence Reconstruction

Reconstruct the following ten sentences by putting the individual words back into their correct order. All of the sentences represent TRUE statements that can be inferred from the information presented in the reading text. Supply appropriate punctuation as needed.

1. and the of in about has poverty massive globalization brought wealth distribution shifts

   ____

   ____

   ____

2. a as of the the into in multiplier banking world comes mechanism through known money money being much

   ____

   ____

   ____

3. in of of out the ninety thin banks air money commercial circulation percent create

____

____

____

4. an of for to in the the it check bank debt money when electronic central certificates government exchange nation's sell needs must U.S.

____

____

____

5. to is is the by the on pay than dollar promise nothing based government's backed U.S. and debt more

____

____

____

6. the the the the interest denomination back than notes accrued designated pay are plus promise more treasury amount government's note nothing of to by

____

____

____

7. had and and years millionaires have ago than billionaires China twenty today more country Russia either far

____

____

____

8. of of to out is the wealthiest Asia world's home today countries eight ten

____

____

____

9. into in on by the the coffers loans earned public public commercial interest a directed lender system is banking back

____

____

____

10. in in to the their is loans for maturity interest full remain best reach borrowers banks' until debt it

____

____

____

LANGUAGE IN USE

PART E

I Suggested Questions for Discussion

A. Briefly describe the different social / economic classes that are most visible in your society. What key features distinguish the lives of the "rich and famous" from those of the "less fortunate"?

B. Describe the overall social attitude toward the poor in your country. What factors are usually cited as being the chief causes of poverty? What is actually being done to alleviate poverty in your society?

C. "Am I my brother's keeper?" In other words, what responsibility does each of us bear, if any, for the welfare of the world's less fortunate?

II Suggested Questions for Written Research Projects

A. Write a report detailing the changes in income disparities in the country of your choice before and after the global economic recession that began in 2007/2008.

B. Write a report describing the overall influence that the "rich and famous" have on your own society. What is the actual source of this influence? How does it affect governmental and/or non-governmental policymaking?

C. Describe and outline your own topic-related research question.

UNIT 7

STOCKS, BONDS, AND WHAT WENT WRONG

BEFORE YOU READ

How do business-savvy people in your country usually invest their money? What types of investments are usually on offer? What types of investments would you personally favor, and which would you normally avoid?

DIRECTIONS: As you read the following text, fill in the numbered blanks with ONE suitable word.

CLOZE TASK

A When states, companies, or other corporate entities need to raise money, either as start-up capital or as a basis for continuing operations or expansion projects, they can adopt any combination of several methods to obtain the desired funds. One [1]____________________ is to borrow money directly from a bank. In times of high liquidity, a company with a sound business plan and earnings history should have no [2]____________ obtaining a bank loan. Another approach is similar to that of issuing IOUs, as briefly described in the previous unit. Corporate IOUs are commonly called bonds.

B There are several different types of bonds. As noted in the previous unit, U.S. treasury bonds have traditionally been considered the "safest" of all investments simply because they carry the backing of the "full faith and credit" of the United States government. Although U.S treasury bonds are deemed a "safer" investment, the [3]________________________ to purchasing them is the low rate of return (or "yield") on the bonds when they are cashed in. One particular type of U.S. government bond carries the designation TIPS, which [4]____________________ for Treasury Inflation Protected Securities. The U.S. Department of the Treasury tracks the respective rate of inflation across six-month periods on the basis of the Consumer Price Index and adjusts the fixed rate of interest return on these securities in [5]____________________ with the calculated inflation rate. One major problem with such "inflation-adjusted" bonds as sold in the United States, however, lies in the major changes introduced by the U.S. government's Bureau of Labor Statistics in the way the inflation rate itself is [6]____________________. The Bureau uses the Consumer Price Index to tabulate the official inflation rate but excludes both food and energy prices from the index, arguing that these are subject to volatile swings and spikes and are thus temporary in nature. Of course for families hit with higher food and transportation costs, the results can be devastating. And when transportation costs rise as a result of geopolitical turmoil and spikes in oil prices, so, [7]____________________, do the costs of all major food items that must be harvested and delivered. It thus hardly seems rational for the government to exclude from its calculations the very core items that have such a profoundly negative effect on the overall purchasing power of working families. In the years that immediately followed the global financial crisis of 2007/2008, numerous economists repeatedly accused the U.S. government of consistently [8]____________________ real inflation numbers.

Image production credit: iStock.com/ Rawpixel

C U.S. treasury notes [9]____________________ from treasury bonds in that the former reach maturity in two, three, five, or ten years, [10]____________________ bonds were originally issued with a maturity range of 30 years. U.S. treasury bills [11]____________________ yet another kind of security with maturities ranging from 4–26 weeks. So-called "munis" or municipal bonds are IOUs issued by municipalities, counties, and states to raise money for vital infrastructural projects. In the United States, munis have traditionally been considered very safe investments, although not quite as secure as bonds or notes backed by the U.S. government itself. Just how precarious municipal bonds may ultimately [12]____________________ out to be became apparent in 2012, when a number of cities across the U.S. began filing for bankruptcy protection.

D Of particular importance during the global financial meltdown that began in 2008 were so-called "agency bonds" issued by Government Sponsored Enterprises (GSEs) like the Federal National Mortgage Association ("Fannie Mae"), the Federal Home Mortgage Corporation ("Freddie Mac"), and the Governmental National Mortgage Association ("Ginnie Mae"), which issued bonds on mortgage securities. (The causal link between the subsequent financial crisis and investment platforms adopted by these GSEs and various financial institutions was also the subject of many heated debates in the U.S. Congress (Cox, 2008).) The GSEs are in effect government-sponsored entities that throughout most of their [13]____________________ were run and operated as private corporate enterprises.

E Corporate bonds are issued by companies and generally [14] ____________________ into two types. Callable bonds permit the issuing company to call in the bond before the debt [15]____________________ maturity if interest rates fall below the rates that were in play at the time the bond was originally [16]____________________. This action would then allow the issuing company to refinance its debt at the preferred lower rate. Convertible bonds, as the name implies, can be [17]____________________ into common stock sold by the company according to terms of sale spelled [18]____________________ by the issuer at the time of purchase.

F Unlike sovereign states and municipalities, companies can also issue stock, enabling share buyers to essentially become part owners of the company. Owning stock in a company has [19]____________________ an upside and a downside. Unlike bonds, [20]____________________ pay out only a fixed sum of accrued principal and interest upon [21]____________________, corporate stocks, which are also known as equities, can actually enable shareholders to reap very large [22] ____________________ if the company's market value goes up. At the same time, shareholders in a company that for whatever reason goes belly up, will lose their entire investment. For this reason, profitable investments in the stock market require a great deal of [23]____________________ into the company's history and general market trends.

G Corporate equities generally fall into two categories: common stocks and preferred stocks. Most people who invest in the stock market [24]____________________ up purchasing common stocks, which give the buyer voting rights in the company. Common stocks are also generally more liquid than preferred shares, meaning that buyers can more readily [25]____________________ them in, with so-called "large-cap" companies often offering buy-sell opportunities on a daily [26]____________. Preferred stock does not normally carry voting rights and is in general far less liquid than the common counterpart. The primary advantage of owning preferred stock lies in the entitlement the holder has to regular dividends. Income from dividends can be especially lucrative with companies that become extremely profitable. In the event of bankruptcy and forced liquidation, bondholders must be paid out first, followed then by those holding preferred stocks, and lastly common stock [27] ____________________.

H Overall trading in the bond markets is roughly three times greater than the volumes traded in stocks. As a general rule, in a bull market for stocks, demand for bonds declines. Conversely, investors who have been burned by falling stock prices in a bear market often seek the perceived safety of [28]____________________.

I Toward the end of the 1990s at the height of the so-called "dot-com" Internet craze, which sent stocks into atmospheric bubbles, a completely new kind of money creation scheme emerged. [29]_____________ up in the brains of "Quantz wizards," i.e., financial analysts specialized in the study of quantitative financial data, this new approach to creating immense wealth was not based on anything real or tangible. The entire scheme was made possible by one key fundamental change in the way banks in the United States had [30]_________________ business since the end of the Great Depression.

J In 1933, the United States Congress passed the Glass-Steagall Act, which was also known as the "Banking Act." Named after its original sponsors, Senator Carter Glass and Representative Henry Steagall, the legislation contained several key provisions that served to regulate the banking industry. One of [31]______________________ provisions drew stark distinctions between the types of banks (commercial lending versus investment) and the means through which they could finance their operations. Glass-Steagall prevented commercial banks from taking the deposits of their clients and using those deposits to engage in investments. But these significant provisions of the legislation were repealed in November of 1999 through passage of the Gramm-Leach-Bliley Act, thus "deregulating" the banking sector and freeing the more aggressive investment sectors of the industry to create increasingly wilder "structured investment vehicles" (SIVs). Nobel laureate Joseph E. Stiglitz (2009) described the repeal of Glass-Steagall most accurately as "the culmination of a $300 million lobbying effort by the banking and financial-services industries" (under point number 2: Tearing Down the Walls).

K One such instrument, hatched [32]_______________ in the higher echelons of hierarchy at JP Morgan Chase (Teather, 2008), went by the [33]________________ BISTRO ("Broad Index Secured Trust Offering"). At the height of the housing craze in the United States, mortgage loans were being given not only to people with no income, no assets, and no jobs, but in some cases even to people whose residence was the local cemetery. Banks, however, were convinced that ownership of the mortgages themselves was a very safe bet and thus transformed the loans themselves into securities.

L As mortgage-backed securities began to be sold, bundled, packaged, and resold, then rebundled, repackaged, and resold yet [34]___________, special structural investment vehicles known as Collateralized Debt Obligations (CDOs) were sold as "over-the-counter derivatives" (Kiff, Elliott, Kazaarian, Scarlata & Spackman, 2009; Lucas, Goodman & Fabozzi, 2006; Weistroffer, 2009) to thousands of insurance companies, investment banks, pension funds, and corporations worldwide. Unimaginable sums of [35]____________________ could be (and were) created through a type of computerized investment wager game known as Credit Default Swaps (Simkovic, 2011). Ownership in companies was not even required in order to reap untold rewards by betting that company ABC would eventually default on its obligations. The cumulative [36]____________________ of these unregulated financial machinations brought the global economic system to the brink of collapse, taking down trillions of dollars in investments, retirement, and savings accounts in the [37]_____________. To explain the true nature of derivatives, financial analyst Max Keiser used the analogy of going into a "house of mirrors" at an amusement park and holding up a one-dollar bill in front of the mirrors. Magically, the bill is [38]____________________ hundreds of times over! At one point, the Bank for International Settlements in Basel, Switzerland, put the total notional value of outstanding global derivatives (including credit default swaps, interest rate, foreign exchange, and commodity derivatives) at 1.5 quadrillion dollars!—in numbers, that is $ 1,500,000,000,000,000,000.

M The only problem was that in the real world of finance, these vast sums of illusionary money were traded and bartered as if they had real substantial value; they didn't. Subsequent investigations of the investment schemes implemented by key investment institutions [39]____________ the truly fraudulent nature of much of this activity. The smoke-and-mirrors game did allow the cream among many financial institutions to reap unimaginable rewards, however. In several important cases, company emails sent among coworkers revealed that financial advisors were actively encouraging clients to invest in these "once-in-a-lifetime" opportunities, while internally laughing at the fools who actually fell for the junk on offer.

N It should be remembered that the enormous, indeed staggering [40]____________________ of money involved in the global financial crisis were created by the banks themselves [41]____________________ of thin air as "special purpose investment vehicles"; in other words, as derivatives. David Stockman (2013), former budget director under the Reagan administration, noted that a full 40% of the entire resources of the United States were committed to "financial objects" with essentially no real benefit to the economy. When the housing bubble popped and the prices of properties all across the U.S. fell from the stratosphere to bargain-basement [42]____________________, the banks demanded that taxpayers themselves replenish these investment houses for the losses incurred through the banks' own wildly speculative investment shenanigans.

Image production credit: iStock.com/KLH49

O The economic crisis that began in 2008 with the collapse of the investment firm Lehman Brothers eventually threatened to [43]__________ a complete global financial meltdown. Lending institutions in many countries suddenly began to tighten their belts by refusing to issue any new credit even to very successful, trustworthy clients and businesses [44] ____________________ big and small. Without credit, thousands of businesses could no longer make critical purchases for vital parts or services in many lines of products, forcing vast numbers of companies to [45]____________________ off increasing numbers of employees. And the people paid the price through lost income, greatly reduced purchasing power, foreclosed homes, obliterated pensions, and long-term unemployment. In several European countries, "austerity measures" were enacted ostensibly to bring each member state's national economy back in line with ideal growth measures by radically curtailing government spending.

P In many families, both husbands and wives joined the ranks of the long-term unemployed, eventually forcing hundreds of thousands of families to lose their homes and savings accounts. Trillions of dollars were lost in the stock market alone as investment portfolios became essentially worthless. Pension funds and other types of retirement accounts, many of [46]__________________ were heavily invested in mortgage-backed securities and other related special purpose vehicles, were also wiped [47]________________, annihilating the lifetime earnings of thousands.

Q Such fates have not been shared by the world's bankers, many of whom awarded themselves tens of millions of dollars in severance pay and bonuses, even as their flagships were sinking. As reported by the *Los Angeles Times* on April 27, 2012, Lehman Brothers had given more than $700 million to its 50 top employees just months before the investment house collapsed in 2008.

R The governments of all G20 nations stepped in to [48] __________ the void created when banks froze credit lines. In the United States, former CEO of Goldman-Sachs, Henry Paulson, who was treasury secretary during the latter part of the George W. Bush administration, warned key members of Congress that there would be martial [49] ______________ in major American cities if the U.S. government failed to do everything in its power to supply the nation's leading banks with the liquidity they needed to start lending again.

S The U.S. government adopted several emergency programs designed to do just [50]____________________. The first of these, which was identified by the acronym TARP (= "Troubled Asset Relief Program"), promised $700 billion in taxpayer money to replenish the coffers of the nation's largest lenders. Through this scheme the U.S. government agreed to relieve leading banks of many of the "toxic assets" held on their accounting books in the form of now worthless mortgage-backed securities and related investments. But much of the money forked over by taxpayers was "parked" at the Federal Reserve, meaning that the banks took the money and redeposited it into their own accounts at the nation's central bank in order to draw interest. Still other banks used the promised support to buy up other wounded lenders. Bank of America bought Wachovia; JP Morgan acquired Bear Stearns and Washington Mutual; and PNC Financial Services took over National City.

T The global economic crisis contributed to a restructuring of society on many levels, and to new formations in governmental power centers, with the people in virtually all countries becoming increasingly suspicious of the global financial elite and of the elected officials who came to the rescue of the bankers.

REFERENCES

Cox, C. (2008, September 23). Testimony concerning turmoil in U.S. credit markets: Recent actions regarding government-sponsored entities, investment banks and other financial institutions. Senate Committee on Banking, Housing, and Urban Affairs.

Kiff, J., Elliott, J., Kazarian, E., Scarlata, J. & Spackman, C. (2009, November). Credit derivatives: Systemic risks and policy options. International Monetary Fund: IMF Working Paper (WP/09/254).

Lucas, D., Goodman, L. & Fabozzi, F. (2006). *Collateralized debt obligations: Structures and analysis*. 2nd edition. New York: John Wiley & Sons Inc.

Simkovic, M. (2011). Leveraged buyout bankruptcies, the problem of hindsight bias, and the credit default swap solution. *Columbia Business Law Review*, *1*, 118.

Stiglitz, J. E. (2009, January). Capitalist fools. *Vanity Fair*, *51*(1).

Stockman, D. (2013). *The great deformation: How crony capitalism corrupted free markets and democracy*. Boston: PublicAffairs / Perseus Books Group.

Teather, D. (2008, September 19). The woman who built financial "weapon of mass destruction." *The Guardian*.

Weistroffer, C. (2009, December 21). Credit default swaps: Heading towards a more stable system. Deutsche Bank Research.

POST-READING QUESTIONS

1. If you were in charge of regulating the banking industry and the stock markets, what changes would you make?
2. Why do some people seem to have an insatiable appetite for a limitless amount of money, though they already have every luxury money can buy?
3. Which would be preferable to you: a job that provides a great deal of work-related satisfaction but only a modest income, or a stressful job with no satisfaction but an enormous income? Why?
4. How would you explain the phrase "Quantz wizards"?
5. Explain the difference between stocks and bonds.
6. In your own words, explain the term "liquidity crisis."
7. How / why did speculative investments lead to the global financial crisis that began in 2007 / 2008?
8. Summarize the most important information presented in this reading. Try not to exceed 500 words.

VOCABULARY WORK

PART A

From the reading text, find the words or phrases that have similar meanings to the words / phrases given in the numbered lists below. The first one has been done for you as an example.

From Paragraphs A–J:	Synonymous Word or Phrase
1. center; middle; heart	core (paragraph B)
2. believed; thought; held to be; presumed	__________
3. erratic; changeable; unstable	__________
4. liquidate; turn into money; exchange	__________
5. sudden increases in price or value	__________
6. monitors (verb); keeps informed of; stays abreast of	__________
7. revenue; profit; income	__________

8. excited; vehement; passionate; worked-up ____________
9. insolvency; ruin; failure ____________
10. a catastrophic collapse of the core elements of something ____________
11. drawback; disadvantage ____________
12. a trading period in stocks characterized by falling share prices ____________
13. a trading period in stocks characterized by rising share prices ____________
14. fail; die out (as a business) ____________
15. supporters; advocates; promoters ____________
16. climax; conclusion; end result; closing ____________
17. glaring; unmistakable; plain; patent; evident ____________
18. specifications; stipulations; terms; clauses; conditions ____________
19. revoked; rescinded; reversed; overturned ____________
20. periods of inflated market prices for specific items or commodities based largely on speculation ____________
21. real; concrete; touchable; physical ____________
22. authorization; empowerment ____________
23. sell-off of a company's assets, for example in a bankruptcy ____________

From Paragraphs K–T: Synonymous Word or Phrase

24. a bet; a gamble ____________
25. tiers or ranks in command or hierarchy ____________
26. at the edge of a steep drop or at a critical juncture ____________

27. an extreme height; a layer of the earth's atmosphere ____________________
28. deceitful tricks; mischievous deeds ____________________
29. trash; worthless garbage ____________________
30. reputedly; supposedly; allegedly ____________________
31. annihilated; destroyed; wiped out ____________________
32. traded in exchange ____________________
33. the top level; the top layer ____________________
34. crooked; dishonest; criminal; shady ____________________
35. restore; refill; resupply ____________________
36. paid for (often unhappily); handed over ____________________
37. funds; a treasury ____________________
38. extra money (besides salary) given to an employee who is leaving a company ____________________
39. cutting back; reducing; decreasing ____________________
40. leery; wary; distrustful; doubting ____________________

PART B

VOCABULARY WORK

Choose an appropriate form of one of the words given below to complete the numbered sentences that follow. Two of the words have been used twice.

BANKRUPT	MELTDOWN
BRINK	OSTENSIBLE
CASH IN	PROVIDE
CULMINATE	REPEAL
DOWNSIDE	SEVERANCE
FRAUD	SPIKE
GO BELLY UP	STARK

1. When businesses ____________________, their assets and inventories are often liquidated at fire sale prices, creating welcome buying opportunities for bargain hunters.

BANKRUPT	MELTDOWN
BRINK	OSTENSIBLE
CASH IN	PROVIDE
CULMINATE	REPEAL
DOWNSIDE	SEVERANCE PAY
FRAUD	SPIKE
GO BELLY UP	STARK

2. The ______________________ of the core of a nuclear reactor constitutes one of the most serious and potentially lethal catastrophes in any country, with long-term effects from radioactive fallout that transcend all national boundaries.

3. Many western banks and other corporations have received strong public criticism for rewarding their parting CEOs with hefty bonuses and ______________________ packages that are, by all rational standards, simply obscene.

4. For most people, the ______________________ differences between the lifestyles of billionaires and those of homeless street people are almost impossible to imagine.

5. Historically, realistic threats of military conflict in the Persian Gulf have caused oil prices to ______________________.

6. After thorough investigation and research trials at a number of medical centers all across the U.S., the claims made by a fairly prominent cancer specialist that he had discovered an extremely effective novel form of treatment were found to be ______________________.

7. Although their true purpose may never be known, the giant stone statues that face out to sea from various points on Easter Island were ______________________ erected to ward off potential invaders arriving by boat.

8. Within days after the United States Supreme Court allowed most of President Obama's national health care law to stand, the president's political opponents vowed to ______________________ the law in Congress.

9. One of the major ______________________ to living in dense urban environments is having to breathe very unhealthy air.

10. Having just lost his job and his home, John was pushed to the ___________ of an emotional breakdown when his wife filed for divorce.

11. After the global financial crisis of 2008, many individuals and companies lost substantial amounts of their net worth and assets, forcing many into ______________________ proceedings.

12. When markets turn sour, many investors often decide to __________ their portfolios, or, in other words, to take the money and run.

13. Gymnast Nadia Comaneci's first-ever scores of perfect 10s during the 1976 Montreal Olympics were the ______________________ of extra-ordinary talent, steely nerves, phenomenal perseverance, countless hours of training, and an insatiable pursuit of perfection.

14. The mass exodus of wealthier citizens and businesses out of southern California will likely ______________________ in substantially reduced tax revenue for the region.

15. The new trade agreement does not include ___________________ for renegotiating labor disputes that will likely arise as a result of outsourcing.

16. Significant ______________________ of the armistice agreement ending World War I dealt with the issue of reparations demanded by France and Great Britain from Germany.

PART C

LANGUAGE FOCUS

1. Find instances of ZERO CONDITIONALS in paragraphs A–D.
2. Find instances of FIRST CONDITIONALS in paragraphs E–F.
3. In paragraphs G–J, find instances of identifying / defining relative clauses.

4. In paragraphs G–J, find instances of non-identifying / non-defining relative clauses.

5. What antecedent noun does the pronoun "they" refer to at the end of the first sentence in paragraph M ". . . they didn't."

Sentence Transformation

For questions 6–10, use the word given below the first sentence to complete the second sentence in the blanks provided. Use between three and eight words including the given word. The given word must NOT be changed in any way, and the meaning of the sentences should be as similar as possible.

Example: We eagerly await a renewed encounter with you in the future.

forward

We are really looking forward to seeing you again in the future.

6. I'm not sure if these shoes are the right size. May I wear them to see if they fit?

   try

   I'm not sure if these shoes are the right size. May I __________________ __________________ to see if they fit?

7. Cynthia must have eaten something that didn't agree with her because she's been vomiting for the last two hours.

   up

   Cynthia must have eaten something that didn't agree with her because she's ______________________________ for the last two hours.

8. My husband is using several social media sites to find the whereabouts of his high school classmates.

   down

   My husband is using several social media sites __________________ __________________ his high school classmates.

9. Your sister has come through the operation very successfully but she's still in critical condition.

   woods

   Your sister has come through the operation very successfully but she's ______________________________ yet.

10. I think Ian simply made the spontaneous decision to invite his bad-tempered neighbors to the block party without considering the consequences.

    spur

    I think Ian simply decided on ______________________ to invite his bad-tempered neighbors to the block party without considering the consequences.

PART D

ULTIMATE CHALLENGE

Sentence Reconstruction

Reconstruct the following ten sentences by putting the individual words back into their correct order. All of the sentences represent TRUE statements that can be inferred from the information presented in the reading text. Supply appropriate punctuation as needed.

1. in do a not stocks stocks common whereas shareholders company preferred usually rights give voting

    ____

    ____

    ____

2. of a by into is out be stock forced liquidation preferred bondholders must followed company shareholders first when paid

    ____

    ____

    ____

3. of to it and the uses prices government from food rates energy U.S. calculate measures inflation excludes the

    ____

    ____

    ____

4. to the in and projects bonds regularly governments desired municipal USA county infrastructure fund issue state

____

____

____

5. that the three than in of is stocks volume of times trading roughly greater bonds

____

____

____

6. in in of to an and demand normally other stand each bonds terms inverse stocks relationship

____

____

____

7. as and of such lost involving through sums credit investment staggering swaps elaborate money default were created derivatives schemes

____

____

____

8. of of to to the the at no mortgage housing height income bubble were source with U.S. issue bankers even encouraged loans people

____

____

____

9. of of to in their the froze response 2008 institutions crisis credit lending economic lines thousands

____

____

____

10. to to to their that were and with no doors services purchase access businesses credit forced needed longer close supplies which had

____

____

____

PART E

LANGUAGE IN USE

I Suggested Questions for Discussion

A. How does the currency in your country come into being? Who / what institution is responsible for issuing the currency, and what steps are involved?

B. Broadly describe the breakdown of monthly income versus expenditures of a typical middle-class family in your country. How have these ratios for identifiable categories such as food and housing changed over the last decade?

C. What types of banking systems exist in your country and what types of services do they provide?

II Suggested Questions for Written Research Projects

A. In several countries, including the United States, a public banking system has been proposed to replace the existing Federal Reserve system. What would be the advantages / disadvantages of a banking system that funneled the interest collected on loans back into the public domain?

B. Discuss the advantages and disadvantages of a currency system based on "hard assets" such as gold or silver.

C. Describe and outline your own topic-related research question.

UNIT 8 ALPHA CITIES AND MEGACITIES

BEFORE YOU READ

Would you prefer to live in a small town / rural community, a medium-size city, or a huge metropolis? Explain why.

DIRECTIONS: As you read the following text, complete the blanks after the numbered brackets with an appropriate form of the word given in capital letters. The first one has been done for you as an example.

CLOZE TASK

A Philosopher Jean-Jacques Rousseau, who was convinced of the essential goodness and educability of the human being, attributed much of the modern malaise he saw in the making to cities—as unsuitable places for human inhabitance. In *Émile*, Rousseau provocatively defined cities as "the abyss of the human species." And that was long before the birth of megacities.

B [0] ARCHEOLOGY archeological evidence dates clusters of human [1] SETTLE____________________ back more than 7,000 years. A few of these towns, such as Athens in Greece, Damascus in Syria, and Jericho in the West Bank, have been [2] CONTINUE____________ inhabited over the millennia. Recent carbon dating of distinctly human artifacts on the west coast of India point to a "lost river civilization" that likely existed there around 7500 BCE.

C Mass urbanization is a relatively new phenomenon, however. The very word "urbanization" and its associated forms is derived from the Latin *urbs*, which meant Rome. In the minds, traditions, and literature of many

Westerners, Rome is the quintessential "Eternal City," the paragon of metropolitan life. The movement of humans from rural landscapes—whether from the steppes of central Asia, the fertile valleys of the Tigris/Euphrates, or the hills and mountains of central China—has tended in one direction. Throughout history, humans have left the often [3] TOLERATE ____________________ hardships experienced on the land to seek better opportunities in "urban" centers. There was, and is, after all, safety in numbers.

D With the onset of [4] INDUSTRY____________________ in England in the eighteenth century, vast numbers of people from rural areas began flooding into cities where they could find work. Watt's steam engine had allowed machines to accomplish tasks in record time on mass scales [5] DREAM____________________ of in previous generations. As both Louis Mumford (1968) and Richard Sennett (1992) have emphasized, in the space of just over 100 years, the population of London had exploded from a mere 150,000 to around 700,000 in 1700. By the middle of the eighteenth century, Paris had also passed the 500,000 mark.

E The people who left their families and familiar [6] SURROUND ____________________ for the promise of a better life in the cities underwent profound mental and emotional changes. Life in rural communities was fairly transparent and relied on the regularity of nature (sunrise, sunset, the beginning of spring, and the onset of autumn), as well as the trust and goodwill of neighbors—and perhaps the extended family—for mutual support. Survival required cooperation and reciprocity.

F In stark contrast, the cities were anonymous jungles in which each man and woman had to fight for [7] SURVIVE____________________. But they also offered the chance to start over in life with a new identity that a person could acquire with just enough street smarts and tenacity. The types of personal transformations that typified the people of this era are [8] MORTAL____________________ in Daniel Dafoe's novel *Moll Flanders*.

G Other metropolises soon followed course in a process that saw dramatic shifts. Today, urbanization is nowhere more pronounced than in

China, where a mass exodus of rural farmers into regional urban hubs of employment opportunities is still underway. In just sixty years, China went from having just five cities with one-million-plus populations to boasting 160 such cities. Often described in the West as the "largest city you've probably never heard of," Chongqing alone has an [9] ADMINISTER ____________________ area population in excess of 32 million, surpassed only by the Tokyo-Yokohama megalopolis with a population of 36 million.

H The extraordinarily rapid growth of China's urban centers has placed heavy demands on the infrastructure, necessitating expansive construction projects for housing, roads, sewers, and water systems to accommodate the masses of newcomers. China's [10] EXPONENT ____________________ economic growth rates on an annual basis have catapulted the country into a global giant of eminent importance. At the same time, the entire Asian-Pacific rim has become the focal point of new markets and technologies. This dramatic shift in the geo-strategic balance of power is also reflected in the status of Asian cities as dynamic hubs of [11] CONNECT____________________ in the global network of industry, finance, and service sectors.

Image production credit: iStock.com/ Oktay Ortakcioglu

I The UK-based "Globalization and World Cities Research Network" (GaWC: www.lboro.ac.uk/gawc) ranked a total of 525 world cities with respect to their importance to 175 key global service firms from the advertising, banking/finance, insurance, law, and management consultancy sectors. Using this matrix with a total of 91,875 service values, the research center found London to be the key global alpha ++ city, accompanied closely by New York. In the words of the research team: "London and New York define a duopoly that constitutes a case apart—'NYLON' is the global cities dyad par excellence."

J But Hong Kong came in third and was described as "approaching the alpha ++ level." And in stark contrast to the results of previous years (2000 and 2004), the "alpha ++ / +" levels are "overrepresented by western Pacific Rim cities (50% in 2000 and 2004), a pattern strongly accentuated in 2008 by the rapid elevation of Sydney, Shanghai and Beijing (THIS IS THE KEY FINDING OF 2008)." [emphasis in the original] (Source: Taylor et al., "Measuring the World City Network: New Results and Developments," Global and World Cities Research Network).

K [12] INDICATE____________________ of the trend and shift in power was the decline of Los Angeles as a world city. Occupying with Chicago a position near the top of the "alpha +" group in 2000, the "City of Angels" dropped to the lower quarter of that column in 2004, and in 2008 occupied a position barely close to the bottom of the "alpha-" category.

L In both 2000 and 2004, Hong Kong, Paris, Tokyo, and Singapore constituted in that order the rank of alpha + cities. But 2008 saw a shift in the importance of two members of this group, with Singapore outranking Tokyo for the first time. The alpha + list also added four new cities: Sydney, Milan, Shanghai, and Beijing. Today, Asian cities like Abu Dhabi, Dubai, Kuala Lumpur, Beijing, Shanghai, and Seoul, are the focus of [13] ARCHITECT ____________________ planning and design teams and of nascent and emerging technologies.

M According to recent United Nations (2012) estimates, by mid-century the total global population residing in cities will exceed seven billion, or a full 70% of the entire population on the planet! Moore & Foster (2011) have reported that China alone plans to set several new records, not the least of which is the creation of the world's largest megacity with a population of 42 million. The gigantic metropolis on the Pearl River Delta will be serviced by twenty-nine rail lines covering 3,100 miles. China also plans to create a number of urban zones with an average of 50 million to 100 million people. The largest of these metropolitan entities—the Bohai Economic Rim—will be home to approximately 260 million people. Good luck finding a parking space there!

Image production credit: iStock.com/bloodua

N The mass concentration of humans in "hypercities" or "megacities" is most clearly seen in nighttime images from space. And indeed, the largest hyper-urban mass of more than 300 million human beings extends from Tokyo through the Korean Peninsula, southward through Beijing, Zhezhang Province, Shanghai, and farther south along the southeast coast of China into Hong Kong and the Pearl River Delta. Similar, though much smaller patterns are visible along the Boston–Washington, D.C. corridor in the United States (approximately 200 million), and in the highly urbanized region that [14] COMPASS ______________________ much of western Europe, including most of England, Belgium, the Netherlands, Luxembourg, Germany, Switzerland, and large parts of France (around 260 million).

O This seemingly [15] STOP______________________ trend toward enormous agglomerations of people in clearly defined regions has brought about two distinctly different visions of what life will look like in these massive urban centers. In the rather sober assessment of the Megacities Foundation, "cities and the regional urbanization process, people coming together to live in dense and regionally connected clusters of activity and built forms, are among the most important forces shaping almost every aspect of human life and societal development" (Soja, 2010, p. 75). A quick look at the data explains why. These vast hyper-urban concentrations of millions upon millions of people are not only the movers and drivers of essentially the entire global economy, they are also the largest consumers of all natural resources and major sources of pollution.

P The rapid globalization of most all aspects of economic and financial activity has also led to gross [16] BALANCE________________ in income and prosperity that threaten social cohesion and [17] GOVERN ______________________. Such disparities "have raised the stakes and heightened the need for effective urban and regional planning, both to take advantage of the positive forces arising from clustering and agglomeration on a regional scale as well as to control the negative effects of increasing income inequality and social polarization. These new developments do not lead simply to a call for creating comprehensive regional planning authorities, as was the case in the past. Today, it may be more necessary than ever before to develop some form of regional governance, but it must be outward looking in the sense of promoting interconnections between major megacity regions and at the same time locally rooted, suggesting some form of confederal structure" (Soja, 2010, p. 75).

Q Particularly in the developing world (but [18] INCREASE ______________________ in the developed world as well), megacities are often [19] CHARACTER______________________ by two or even three grossly disparate worlds living in close juxtaposition to one another. Urban theorist Mike Davis (2006) exposed the often horrendous living conditions faced by millions of the destitute migrants who either have grown up in the abject squalor of shantytowns and mega-slums within or on the [20] SKIRT______________________ of many megacities—in Mumbai, Cairo, Dhaka, Khartoum, Kolkata, Cape Town, Mexico City, Manila, Caracas, Sao Paolo, and Jakarta—or have migrated there in the hope of finding viable employment. The economic preconditions that once existed during the mass urbanization phases of previous eras no longer exist. Children who are born and come of age in these "stinking mountains of shit," have very little hope of ever becoming integrated into the spheres of the jet-setter elite who reside within the [21] PROTECT____________________ bounds of private armies inside gated communities. Instead, they live in an underworld economy of prostitution, drug smuggling, bank [22] ROB____________________, [23] EXTORT____________________, and the trade in human donor organs. In many cities of the world, wealthier [24] INHABIT____________________ must travel either by helicopter or in bullet-proof limousines with armed guards to avoid being kidnapped for ransom or killed.

R In a very [25] LIGHT____________________ review of Davis's *Planet of Slums*, author Pepe Escobar provided background information on the types of organized violence that continue to plague Sao Paulo, Brazil. One of the most notorious of these violent organizations, the "First Capital Command" (Primeiro Comando da Capital), a "super-gang" that controls "most of Sao Paulo's overcrowded and notoriously corrupt prisons ... declared war against Brazil's wealthiest state. From inside their prison cells, using U.S. $150 mobile phones, they ordered motorcyclist 'bin Ladens'—warriors indebted to the PCC, heavily armed with guns, shotguns, hand grenades, machine guns and Molotov cocktails—to conduct a violent orgy: spraying police cars with bullets, hurling grenades at police stations, attacking officers in their homes and after-hours hangouts, torching dozens of buses (after passengers had been ordered off), and robbing banks. Almost 100 people were killed in three days. On Monday, the PCC managed single-handedly to virtually paralyze Sao Paulo, the third-largest of the world's hypercities (those with more than 19 million people)" (Escobar, 2006, para. 1 and 2).

S The scenes Escobar has described conjure up images of a country at the brink of collapse or civil war. It is indeed difficult to imagine what measures can be taken to lift hundreds of millions of people out of poverty and to educate them in valuable skills that might offer them a much brighter future. But history teaches us significant lessons: when countless masses of people rise up, there is little that can be done to stop them. Millions of people living in squalid poverty constitute a potential powder keg capable of bringing even the most highly organized society to its knees.

T But perhaps a concerted global effort to create a more balanced playing field offers a glimmer of hope. Already, urban planners around the world are hard at work designing sustainable communities that might one day allow their residents to live in greater harmony with nature, while using far fewer of the earth's precious natural resources. Green technologies might enable megacities to feed all their inhabitants without destroying environmentally sensitive ecosystems in the process. At the same time, a recent paper authored by Desmet and Rossi-Hansberg (2012) warned of the enormous complexity involved in attempts to restrict the growth of megacities. The study points out that cities are in fact complex systems with an inherent dynamic, so that changes in one component can have profound and often unforeseen consequences in others: "When analyzing whether mega-cities have become 'too large,' policy makers often focus on an in-depth analysis of a particular city, such as Mexico City, Cairo, or Shanghai. However, no city is an island: improving urban infrastructure in one city may attract immigration from other cities, and a negative shock in one location may be mitigated because people can move to another location. Considering the general equilibrium nature of any such scale-dependent urban policy is therefore key. That is, when deciding whether to make intermediate-sized cities more attractive, policy makers need to understand how that will affect both smaller and larger cities" (Desmet & Rossi-Hansberg, 2012, p. 2).

U One thing is for certain: in the not too distant future, we will come to learn—one way or the other—just how many people planet Earth is capable of supporting.

REFERENCES

Davis, M. (2006). *Planet of Slums*. NY / London: Verso.

Desmet, K. & Rossi-Hansberg, E. (2012). Analyzing urban systems: Have mega-cities become too large? Princeton University. Retrieved April 18, 2015, from http://www.princeton.edu/~erossi/WBChapterKD%26ERH.pdf.

Escobar, P. (2006, May 20). The accumulation of the wretched. [Review of the book *Planet of Slums*, by M. Davis]. *Asia Times*. Retrieved June 22, 2014, from http://www.atimes.com/atimes/Front_Page/HE20Aa01.html

Moore, M. & Foster, P. (2011, January 24). China to create largest mega city in the world with 42 million people. *The Telegraph*. Retrieved November 16, 2014 from http://www.telegraph.co.uk/news/worldnews/asia/china/8278315/China-to-create-largest-mega-city-in-the-world-with-42-million-people.html

Mumford, L. (1968). *The city in history: Its origins, its transformations, and its prospects*. NY: Mariner Books.

Sennett, R. (1992). *The fall of public man*. New York: W. W. Norton.

Soja, E. (2010). Regional urbanization and the future of megacities. In: Hall, P., Buijs, S., Tan, W., Tunas, D. *Megacities – Exploring a sustainable future*. Rotterdam: 010 Publishers. pp. 57–75.

United Nations. (2012). World Urbanization Prospects. The 2011 Revision.

POST-READING QUESTIONS

1. Did your view of city life versus small-town or rural life change while reading the text?
2. If you could choose any place in the world to live for the next 10 years, where would that be?
3. In your view, what is the nicest city or town in your country and why would you recommend it as a tourist destination?
4. What are the advantages of city life over the small-town environment?
5. What are the advantages of living in the countryside versus living in a large city?
6. Explain how rapid urbanization in eighteenth century Europe affected individuals and how it created a new type of citizen.
7. In your own words, describe the mundane world of the destitute in many hyper-urban regions of the developing world.
8. Describe the challenges posed by megacities.

VOCABULARY WORK

PART A

From the reading text, find the words or phrases that have similar meanings to the words / phrases given in the numbered lists below. The first one has been done for you as an example.

From Paragraphs A–I:	Synonymous Word or Phrase
1. give and take; mutuality; interchange	reciprocity (paragraph E)
2. shrewdness to survive or succeed in any kind of environment or situation	____________
3. periods lasting 1,000 years	____________
4. an object or tool made by human beings	____________
5. persistence; perseverance; endurance; stamina	____________
6. misfortunes; difficulties; adverse circumstances	____________
7. prototypical; being the perfect embodiment of something	____________
8. groups; aggregates; collections	____________
9. perfect model or ideal of something	____________
10. vast plains of grasslands	____________
11. of prominent, high rank or importance	____________
12. drainage pipes or channels for waste water and refuse	____________
13. flight or departure from a place, often on a mass scale; emigration	____________
14. a person or firm with an advisory function	____________
15. focal points; centers of activity; convergence points	____________

From Paragraphs J–U:	Synonymous Word or Phrase
16. stressed; highlighted; emphasized	____________
17. budding; beginning; developing	____________
18. imparities; inequalities	____________
19. the condition or state of being placed side by side	____________

20. extensive; inclusive; expansive ____________
21. workable; practicable ____________
22. clusters; groups; collections ____________
23. dirty; miserably degraded; foul ____________
24. an inkling; a flicker; a twinkle ____________
25. a container of explosive material; (figuratively: a potentially explosive situation) ____________
26. invoke ____________
27. money paid to kidnappers in exchange for a person or thing of value ____________
28. lacking means for food and clothing; impoverished ____________
29. criminal domains of society ____________
30. famous in a negative way; infamous; disreputable; ill-famed ____________

VOCABULARY WORK

PART B

Choose an appropriate form of one of the words given below to complete the numbered sentences that follow. Two of the words have been used twice.

CLUSTERS	NOTORIETY
COMPREHEND	PARAGON
CONJURE UP	RECIPROCAL
CONSULT	SEWER
DESTITUTE	STREET SMARTS
HARDSHIP	TENACITY
HEIGHT	VIABLE

1. Until well after the time of Newton, Aristotelian logic served as the ____________ of deductive reasoning.

2. The ____________ endured by many of the families of the Dust Bowl era are touchingly recounted in John Steinbeck's *The Grapes of Wrath*.

3. With extremely poor eyesight, bats rely on a greatly ______________ sense of hearing and an elaborate internal system of echolocation for survival.

4. Tennis legend Monica Seles enjoyed a reputation for being one of the most ________________________ players ever to master the game, playing every single point as if it was match point and never giving her opponents any reprieve from a seemingly endless series of blasted groundstrokes.

5. What is believed to be the world's oldest toilet and _______________ system dating back to 764 BCE was unearthed in the Turkish province of Van.

6. High-end digital cameras of 50 MP and more have established themselves as ________________________ alternatives to traditional film cameras and as particularly flexible instruments in the hands of professional photographers.

7. Born to an inmate mother in Newgate prison, Daniel Dafoe's title character Moll Flanders not only survived in London through her beguiling charm and wily ________________________, but also went on to become impressively wealthy.

8. Financial ________________________ advise clients on a wide range of investment options to protect and expand the client's wealth.

9. Instead of treating isolated, specific symptoms of illness, holistic medicine adopts a ________________________ approach to the biological body as a functional whole.

10. During the Dust Bowl era of the 1930s, many of America's farmers were left ________________________ as the relentless drought turned their once fertile farmland into barren dust, forcing thousands of families into homelessness and hunger.

11. ________________________ for his apparently insatiable sexual drive, Mongolian conqueror Genghis Khan passed on his genes to an estimated 16 million descendants.

CLUSTERS	NOTORIETY
COMPREHEND	PARAGON
CONJURE UP	RECIPROCAL
CONSULT	SEWER
DESTITUTE	STREET SMARTS
HARDSHIP	TENACITY
HEIGHT	VIABLE

12. In everyday dealings with others, individuals in collectivist agricultural societies tend to rely on long-standing traditions of __________________ rather than on codified prescriptive contracts.

13. Pictures of the Great Pyramids of Giza always __________________ images of Cleopatra, King Tut, and a host of other iconic symbols of the once great ancient civilization.

14. Different types of industrial/technological research and development centers tend to occur in ______________________ in various countries, such as information technology centers in Boston and Silicon Valley in the USA; Hsinchu Science Park in Taiwan; Samsung Town in Seoul, South Korea; Kansai Science City in Japan; Bangalore in India; Dalian Hi-Tech Zone and Jiaxing Software Park in China; the Technologie Zentrum Chemnitz and the Dresden Centers of computer technology in Germany; and in dozens of decentralized research centers spread through-out France and other countries.

15. Texas-based radio host Alex Jones gained widespread _____________ for his vehement opposition to globalization in almost every form.

16. When school children disrupt normal classroom instruction or become aggressive or violent, counselors and psychologists usually bring in the parents of the students for ______________________.

LANGUAGE FOCUS

PART C

1. Identify the noun that the pronoun "they" refers to in the second sentence of paragraph F.

2. List the superlative adjectives found in the paragraphs M–R (e.g., "fastest," "slowest," "smallest," etc.)

3. In paragraphs M–P, identify present participles used in reduced relative clauses.

4. List examples in the text of Greek or Latin roots affixed to English adjectives or nouns to create a new concept (e.g., "*mega*-cities").

5. What phrase could best replace "when countless masses of people rise up" in paragraph S?

Sentence Transformation

For questions 6–10, use the word given below the first sentence to complete the second sentence in the blanks provided. Use between three and eight words including the given word. The given word must NOT be changed in any way, and the meaning of the sentences should be as similar as possible.

Example: We eagerly await a renewed encounter with you in the future.
forward
We are really looking forward to seeing you again in the future.

6. Having to obey someone who is narcissistic and mean-spirited is not something most of us relish.
orders
Having ________________________________ someone who is narcissistic and mean-spirited is not something most of us relish.

7. To resolve all the bugs in this program, we're going to have to start over from the very beginning.
scratch
To resolve all the bugs in this program, we'll be forced ____________ ________________________________.

8. Take my advice: apply for promotion now, otherwise you're going to be left empty-handed.
cold
Take my advice: apply for promotion now, otherwise you're going to ________________________________.

9. The amendments to the labor agreement were ultimately very detrimental to the work force.

   turned

   The amendments to the labor agreement ______________________
   ______________________ very detrimental to the work force.

10. I'd strongly advise you to consider their proposal very carefully before giving your written consent.

    dotted

    I'd strongly advise you to consider their proposal very carefully ______________________ line.

ULTIMATE CHALLENGE

PART D

Sentence Reconstruction

Reconstruct the following ten sentences by putting the individual words back into their correct order. All of the sentences represent TRUE statements that can be inferred from the information presented in the reading text. Supply appropriate punctuation as needed.

1. it in the the with urbanization Age recorded Europe mass first Industrial brought

   ____
   ____
   ____

2. of in to centers economic many has urban led rapid rates China development growth exponential

   ____
   ____
   ____

3. and in the the of the of in many dramatically Australia importance Pacific power increased balance toward shifts western Asia have cities

4. in of a of be the will are this centers century population that urban seventy earth's predictions living percent middle by full

5. the the on in of environment infrastructure enormous concentrations and place mass demands humans both megacities

6. are be and to the of water energy self-sustaining designed sources being renewable recycling largely eco-cities systems use through

7. the the the in in to of world urban led between centers increased rich stark developing many have income ghettoization disparities poor and

8. for to of of the the in impoverished developing confronting society's provide areas planners major necessities world officials and one urban how life is government problem many

9. in to of our cities natural function today the that planners environment harmony create goal with is primary urban greater

____

____

____

10. do to and that are not technologies damage communities helping friendly ecosystems sensitive sustainable materials environmentally developers construct

____

____

____

LANGUAGE IN USE

PART E

I Suggested Questions for Discussion

A. Describe some of the most important or renowned features of two of the most populous cities in your country. Include information about their history, physical layout or design, and primary attractions.

B. Describe the largest city you've ever visited or lived in. What did (or do) you like about it, and what did (or do) you dislike?

C. What character trait differences have been attributed to the different native populations of the various cities or regions in your country? (For example, New Yorkers enjoy a reputation in the United States for being fast-talking, fast-walking, and unabashedly direct in their communication style.)

II Suggested Questions for Written Research Projects

A. What are the major factors limiting urban growth, and is there an upper limit on the population size that a megacity can support?

B. How do the ever-increasing sizes of urban centers affect the lifestyle and the quality of life of the inhabitants?

C. Describe and outline your own topic-related research question.

ENGINEERING MARVELS

UNIT 9

BEFORE YOU READ

Describe the most impressive house, building, or structure you have seen based on its architecture and aesthetic appeal.

DIRECTIONS: As you read the following text, fill in the numbered blanks with ONE suitable word.

CLOZE TASK

A The twenty-first century has already witnessed [1]____________ can only be described as a revolution in architecture and civil engineering. New processes coupled with ultra-high-strength materials have made possible the creation of structures [2]____________________ considered unthinkable. Many of these superstructures incorporate state-of-the-art computer technology that allows for the intelligent control of many critical functions to dramatically [3]__________________ energy consumption and waste. At the same time, the development of entire series of supercomputers has enabled science to explore regions of the cosmos and questions surrounding the nature of physical reality that would have been all but unimaginable a century ago.

B By far the most sophisticated machine complex ever [4]__________ by human hands and minds is CERN's Large Hadron Collider. Straddling the border of Switzerland and France near Geneva, the LHC is the world's largest and most powerful particle accelerator, capable of [5]___________ enough energy to send trillions of protons in opposite directions around a

27 km ring at 99.99% the speed of light. Each particle packs the power-punch of seven TeV (tera-electronvolts). Every second, some 600 million collisions of 14 TeV each generate temperatures 100,000 times hotter than those at the core of the sun. The ring system itself, equipped with 9,300 magnets, is enclosed in an elaborate "cryogenic distribution system" in which liquid helium is constantly circulated at [6]____________________ just above absolute zero or -273.16 °C. Annually, the 15 petabytes of data (1 petabyte = 1 million gigabytes) produced by these vast numbers of collisions would completely fill 1.7 million dual-layer DVDs.

Image production credit: iStock.com/xenotar

C The [7]____________________ of this vast complex is to simulate as closely as possible the energies that are believed to have existed shortly after the Big Bang. Many researchers posited from early on that at even lower energies it might be possible to obtain evidence of the hypothesized Higgs Boson (a.k.a. the "God particle"). Without the Higgs, [8]____________________ would be very hard pressed to explain in terms of the Standard Model how and why particles have mass at all.

D And indeed, on July 4, 2012, before an audience of hundreds (including Peter Higgs himself) and millions more tuned in worldwide via Internet connection and television screens, CERN's CMS (Compact Muon Solenoid) team of physicists [9]____________________ that they had amassed (no pun intended) an overwhelming amount of evidence that the Higgs had quite probably been [10]____________________ at 125.3 giga-electronvolts (GeV). This would mean that the particle is 133 times heavier than a proton. (More detailed information on the work of CERN's CMS team can be found at their website: http://cms.web.cern.ch/)

E The data obtained by the LHC had to pass physicists' 5-Sigma certification requirements for any discovery. A sigma-5 level discovery would approximate the statistical [11]____________________ of having a coin toss turn up tails 20 times in a row, signifying that a principle other than chance has to be assumed in any explanation. This degree of [12]____________________ requires a great deal of usable data. At the time of CERN's announcement, the usable data they had obtained had already been given a 4.9-sigma rating, indicating a one in two million likelihood that a new particle had been found. The question was: was it truly the Higgs?

F To solve the extraordinarily complex task of sifting [13] ____________________ the unprecedented amounts of data, CERN established the Worldwide LHC Computing Grid (WLCG), a multi-national collaboration [14] ____________________ literally thousands of scientists in more than 30 countries. This allows for the global distribution of all experimental data to 11 larger computer centers designated as "Tier 1" in various parts of the world. The Tier 1 centers subsequently distribute the data further through a much more [15]________________ network of 160 "Tier 2" processing centers. (Interested readers can discover more about all aspects of the Large Hadron Collider at: http://public.web.cern.ch/public/en/lhc/lhc-en.html)

G The effort paid off. The painstaking analysis of the mountain of data revealed that the discovered spinless boson conformed precisely to the patterns predicted by the Standard Model. The Nobel Committee rightfully awarded the Nobel Prize in Physics for 2013 to Peter W. Higgs and to François Englert "for the theoretical discovery of a mechanism that contributes to our understanding of the origin of mass of subatomic particles, and which recently was confirmed through the discovery of the predicted fundamental particle, by the ATLAS and CMS experiments at CERN's Large Hadron Collider." And the world of theoretical physics breathed an enormous sigh of relief.

H But also in the more mundane world of housing and office complexes, the twenty-first century has heralded a number of interesting breakthroughs. In the southwestern United States, "earthships" have redefined "recycling" for the housing [16]____________________. These beautiful and environmentally friendly homes are [17]____________________ using very little outside of worn-out car tires that would normally be burned as junk, empty soft drink cans made of aluminum, and soil or sand readily available in the surrounding environment. The tires are placed in [18]____________________ that largely mimic traditional brick-and-mortar structures with the voids between the tires occupied by beverage cans filled with sand. The thick walls have a very high thermal mass, [19]____________________ the inside of the structure cool in the summer and warm in the winter. Many of these novel houses also have south-facing winter gardens equipped with gray-water recycling systems. Rainwater is collected in large tanks, supplying the occupants with all the water they need. Large areas of solar panels usually fixed to the roofs qualify the homes as "off-the-grid" listings.

I The trend toward self-sufficiency is also visible in the design of both larger apartment complexes and entire cities, as China's first mass-scale eco-city in Tianjin demonstrates. Designed for 350,000 residents, Eco-City plans incorporate seven different areas [20]____________________ from an Eco-Valley and a Lifescape to an Earthscape and a Solarscape, all employing the newest earth-friendly technologies. [21]____________________ on wind and solar power, integrated waste water recycling and seawater desalination systems, the haute-design city is largely self-sustaining.

J In [22]____________________ of construction costs and the challenges [23]____________________ with the entire building process, China's Three Gorges Dam stands alone in a category of its own. The price tag for the mammoth undertaking has been listed at between \$26 billion and \$30 billion. With a length of 2,335 m, a height of 185 m, and a base [24]____________________ of 115 m, the massive dam controls a reservoir area of 1045 km^2, and generates annually 80,000 GWh of [25]____________________. The dam is [26]____________________ with 28 turbines capable of producing 700 MW each, and two 50 MW generators. Its spillway capacity is a staggering 116,000 m^3/sec.

Image production credit: iStock.com/xenotar

K Construction of the dam required 463,000 tons of steel and 200,000 m^3 of concrete. Approximately 102,600,000 m^3 of earth was displaced in the construction process. For more information on the Three Gorges Dam, visit the corporate website at: http://www.ctgpc.com.cn/en

L The past two decades have also seen the emergence of skyscrapers of truly dizzying [27]______________________: Burj Khalifa in Dubai; Taipei 101; the Shanghai World Financial Center; and the International Commerce Centre in Hong Kong.

Image production credit: iStock.com/dblight

M Upon completion in 2010, Dubai's Burj Khalifa succeeded in shattering all previous records, and not only with its dazzling height of 828 meters and 163 floors. Designed by Skidmore, Owings and Merrill of Chicago (USA), the building boasts the world's highest (at the top of the building) and fastest elevators (64 km/h); the highest nightclub on the 144th floor; the highest restaurant at 442 meters; and the highest open-space observation platform on the 124th floor. Over 100 km of [28] ____________________ carry on average 940,000 liters of water daily. The foundation of the building contains 110,000 tons of concrete, reinforced with 1.5 m thick steel piles of 43 m lengths set at a depth of 50 m. The total construction required 330,000 m^3 of a special mix of concrete designed to [29]____________________ the temperature extremes common during the scorching Dubai summers. Readers can take a virtual tour of the Burj Khalifa at the building's website: http://www.burjkhalifa.ae

N In the race to the top, the sky is apparently the [30]____________. Not to be outdone by its neighbor to the southeast, Saudi Arabia announced in 2011 the construction of the newest "world's tallest building" with the eminent title "Kingdom Tower." Designed by the Chicago-based architectural firm Adrian Smith + Gordon Grill (AS + GG), the building was originally planned to tower a full mile high into the sky, or the equivalent of 1.6 km. Studies of soil conditions at the construction [31]____________________ cast doubt on whether the ground could in fact support a structure of that size, so the building had to be downsized somewhat. With 12 escalators, 59 elevators, one of which travels at 36 km/h to and from the observatory, and a 30 m sky terrace on the 157th level, the design encompasses 530,000 m^2. The $1.2 billion Kingdom Tower is only the tallest central feature of an entire complex known as "Kingdom City," north of Jeddah on the Red Sea. The triangular-shaped Kingdom Tower is designed to take full advantage of the complex wind conditions along the coast by employing tapered wings along its sides.

O Because of the complex engineering involved, Tokyo's Sky Tree is in at least one important respect even more impressive than the Kingdom Tower. As is well known, Japan lies at the juncture of several tectonic plates. The March 2011 massive shift westward of the Pacific plate under the Eurasian mass caused a magnitude 9.0 earthquake and generated a devastating tsunami that destroyed much of the northeastern coast of Honshu. Japanese engineers must always consider the worst-case scenario of a massive earthquake and tsunami hitting the foundations of any structure erected [32]____________________ the coast. Because of the complex waves generated by earthquakes, many factors must be carefully [33]____________________ when any type of building is constructed in such seismically active zones. Highly elaborate algorithms fed into fast computers allow engineers and architects to simulate ground [34] ____________________ and its effects on buildings of various shapes, dimensions, and configurations.

Image production credit: iStock.com/Torsakarin

P Completed in February of 2012 and opened to the public on May 22, 2012, the gracefully majestic Sky Tree towers 634 m above the Tokyo skyline. With a total [35]____________________ of 40 billion Japanese Yen (or 440 million U.S. dollars), the Sky Tree was designed to provide broadcasting services for nine television and several radio stations. The tower also contains an elaborate restaurant and an observation deck of a very unusual design. Visitors ascend to the top accessible level via a spiral glass skywalk. One section of the walk features a glass floor, allowing for a breathtaking [36]____________________ of the streets directly below.

Q One especially remarkable [37]____________________ of Tokyo's Sky Tree is its distinct resemblance to the traditional Japanese pagoda. True marvels of engineering in their [38]____________________ right, pagodas have stood the test of [39]____________________, despite their fragile, flimsy appearance. As *The Economist* (1997) aptly put it, pagodas are an "engineering mystery." Of the approximately 500 pagodas found in Japan, a few of which date back to the seventh century, not one has suffered major damage in an earthquake, despite the fact that Japan is one of the most seismically active places on the [40]________________. Over the past 1,400 years, the country most likely will have been hit not only by untold numbers of powerful temblors, but also by fierce typhoons with potentially destructive winds. But the pagodas have stood essentially unfazed by nature's fury.

R Scientists have only recently begun to unravel the secrets of these mysterious structures. The traditional five-story pagoda is constructed using nothing but timber, wooden pegs, wedges, and clay tiles. Each floor is staggered and offset in [41]__________________ to the one above and the one below it. And in contrast to pagodas found in both China (where the structural design originated) and Korea, the Japanese versions are [42] ________________ by eaves that extend much farther out from each wall.

S It was long believed that the large and important central column, known in Japanese as the *shinbashira*, played the most significant [43]____________________ in holding the buildings up in violent earthquakes; but in fact, in quite a number of pagodas, the central mast is not even connected to the ground, but rather left dangling from the top of the structure. The strongest, however, dating back from the earliest phases of Japanese pagoda construction, do reportedly have the central column anchored into the ground.

T Detailed studies of the buildings show that the [44]____________ of the structures is always carried by 12 sturdy outer beams (known in Japanese as the *Gawa-bashira*) along the sides of the outer square, and by additional masts or columns (the *Shiten-bashira*) on the perimeter of the interior square. Astonishingly, none of these vital weight-bearing beams extends vertically through the height of the building in such a way that each floor would be connected. As *The Economist* pointed out in its article on the mysteries of pagodas, "the individual storeys are not actually attached to one another. They are simply stacked one on top of another like a pile of hats. What joints there are between the floors are loosely fitting wooden brackets that allow each storey to slither around" (paragraph 12). The buildings themselves are enormously stable, but at the same time elastic enough to allow them to sway back and [45]____________________ as the ground shakes beneath them. Several recent studies (Hanazato, Fujita, Sakamoto, Inayama & Ohkura, 2004; Tanimura & Ishida, 1997) have confirmed [46] ____________________ many engineers have long suspected: the central column acts "as a mass damper during severe earthquakes." In other [47]____________________, the ground motion is in effect counter-balanced by the inertia of the central column and the individual floors moving asynchronously with each [48]_____________. Other studies [49]____________________ by Tanimura & Ishida have also shown that the central column of the pagoda effectively disperses the energy resulting from the rocking motion of the sides, while individual floors counteract the lateral movement of the respective floors above and below. This same principle of seismic engineering has been employed in a number of high-tech buildings throughout Japan, Taiwan (including Taipei 101), and the west coast of the United States.

U What remains baffling, however, is how early Japanese carpenters from the 7th and 8th centuries could have constructed such an astonishingly sophisticated structure, which maintains its [50]_____________ integrity in the face of much that nature throws at it.

V As materials science advances our understanding of new alloys, polymers, nano-scale meta-materials, and plastics, newer product designs with astounding structural properties are coming into view. These products are gradually making their way into the mainstream design studios and are beginning to form the basis of elaborate expressions of architecture that would have been unthinkable to previous generations.

REFERENCES

The Economist. (1997, December 18). An engineering mystery. Why pagodas don't fall down. Retrieved November 20, 2014 from http://www.economist.com/node/456070

Hanazato, T., Fujita, K., Sakamoto, I., Inayama, M. & Ohkura, Y. (2004). Analysis of earthquake resistance of five-storied timber pagoda (paper no. 1223). Paper presented at the 13th World Conference on Earthquake Engineering, Vancouver, B. C., Canada.

Tanimura, A. & Ishida, S. (1997). Energy dispersion and dissipation mechanism of a Shinbashira-Frame system. *Journal of Structural Engineering. B*, (*43*)B, 143–150.

POST-READING QUESTIONS

1. Which of the man-made structures described in the text would you most like to visit? Why?
2. Which of the structures described in the text do you believe is the best tourist attraction? Why?
3. Can you imagine living in a skyscraper 500 m above the ground? Why or why not?
4. What is the most frequently visited building or monument in your country?
5. How would you describe the Japanese pagodas' earthquake-resistant features to someone who hasn't read the text?
6. In your own words, describe the special features of CERN's LHC.
7. Explain how new types of materials have contributed to new forms of architecture.
8. In your own words, describe the unusual structural properties of Japanese pagodas.

VOCABULARY WORK

PART A

From the reading text, find the words or phrases that have similar meanings to the words / phrases given in the numbered lists below. The first one has been done for you as an example.

From Paragraphs A–K:	Synonymous Word or Phrase
1. theorized; postulated	hypothesized (para C)
2. enveloped; ringed by; circumvallated	____________________
3. together with; joined with	____________________
4. sent around; spread around	____________________
5. watched; viewed	____________________
6. existing in a concrete, material form	____________________
7. gaps; empty spaces	____________________
8. appear; manifest itself; present itself	____________________
9. in succession; in series	____________________
10. sudden significant advances in science, technology, medicine, etc.	____________________
11. residents; inhabitants	____________________
12. a type of rotor machine with blades or vanes that is driven by an air or water current	____________________
13. integrate; include; encompass	____________________
14. a process of removing salt from seawater	____________________
15. gigantic	____________________

From Paragraphs L–V:	Synonymous Word or Phrase
16. breaking; surpassing	____________________
17. meeting point; intersection	____________________
18. made smaller; reduced in height or size	____________________
19. gradually narrowed; slimmed	____________________
20. searing hot	____________________
21. structures; external forms; figures	____________________
22. climb; scale; move upward	____________________

23. rickety; delicate ____________________

24. tremors; earthquakes ____________________

25. (figuratively): violence; ferocity; brute force ____________________

26. hanging down; swinging ____________________

27. soundness; intactness ____________________

28. to slide back and forth sideways like a snake ____________________

29. happening at different times ____________________

30. belonging to the dominant, standard, or principally accepted version of something ____________________

31. dissipates; spreads out; scatters ____________________

VOCABULARY WORK

PART B

Choose an appropriate form of one of the words given below to complete the numbered sentences that follow. Two of the words have been used twice.

ASYNCHRONOUS	HYPOTHESIS
BREAKTHROUGH	IN A ROW
BRICK-AND-MORTAR	INCORPORATE
DANGLE	INTEGRATE
DOWNSIZE	MAINSTREAM
ENCLOSE	OCCUPY
FEND	TURN UP

1. It seems natural in sprawling metropolises such as Los Angeles that many residents would prefer to shop online as opposed to spending an hour driving to a traditional ____________________ store, only to discover that the item is out of stock and would need to be ordered.

2. The discovery of the quantum mechanical nature of matter's most fundamental particles constituted a truly momentous ____________________ in the human quest to understand the world we live in.

3. The odds of winning a major jackpot in the lottery are infinitesimally small, but one person's winning three times ____________________ is simply phenomenal.

4. The long-term plan of leading visionaries is to ____________________ all of the Middle East and Northern Africa into a political-economic union with Europe.

5. Moral ________________________ consists of far more than merely following the letter of the law; it also entails treating others as you would want them to treat you, and viewing all others as ends unto themselves rather than as instruments for personal gain.

6. For children in many northern European societies, the passage out of childhood has traditionally been deemed a critical juncture in life when young adults assume the responsibilities of earning their own living and ________________________ for themselves.

7. The genetic material of a virus is normally completely ____________ within an outer protein coating, and in some strains also an external envelope.

8. Corporate ________________________ has become a euphemistic synonym for laying off large numbers of employees.

9. Freud ________________________ that the human psyche consisted of three functional domains, which he designated the id, the ego, and the superego.

10. The film star wore a flattering azure evening gown that was nicely complemented by a slew of sparkling sapphires ______________________ from her ears.

11. Hard copies of academic job applications should never contain letters of reference ________________________ within the same envelope. Today, the widespread use of email attachments has made hard copies and "snail mail" practically obsolete anyhow.

12. In many countries around the world, illegal ____________________ of buildings are often forcibly evicted by the police.

13. In a great many disciplines, academic researchers experience quite early in their careers the tacit pressure to conform to ______________________ thought; mavericks with unorthodox views are often weeded out early in the job selection process.

ASYNCHRONOUS	IN A ROW
BREAKTHROUGH	INCORPORATE
BRICK-AND-MORTAR	INTEGRATE
DANGLE	FEND
DOWNSIZE	MAINSTREAM
ENCLOSE	OCCUPY
HYPOTHESIS	TURN UP

14. Evidence of malicious code or computer malware does not always ______________________ the first time the infected program is launched.

15. Albert Einstein recognized the special place that Johann Sebastian Bach ____________________ in the history of music when the physicist remarked that when God created the universe, Bach wrote the musical score.

16. Patterns of economic development in northern and in southern Europe have been marked by a fairly high degree of ____________________, with much of northern Europe characterized by a rational-bureaucratic state apparatus and advanced levels of industrialization, while southern Europe has been reliant on a decentralized collectivist framework typical of agricultural societies.

LANGUAGE FOCUS

PART C

1. Identify the noun clauses and their functions in paragraphs C and D.

2. What does the word "This" refer to at the beginning of the second sentence in paragraph F?

3. Identify the main sentence subject and the main sentence verb in the second sentence in paragraph I.

4. Identify the verb tense and voice used predominately in paragraph H. In which other parts of the text is this tense/voice used? Why?

5. How do you say the term "m^3"? How do you say the term "m^2"?

Sentence Transformation

For questions 6–10, use the word given below the first sentence to complete the second sentence in the blanks provided. Use between three and eight words including the given word. The given word must NOT be changed in any way, and the meaning of the sentences should be as similar as possible.

Example: We eagerly await a renewed encounter with you in the future.
forward
We are really looking forward to seeing you again in the future.

6. After a year's worth of declining sales, the company is now near collapse.
verge
The company is now ________________________________
after a year's worth of declining sales.

7. The final 2,000 m of the climbers' descent was especially uncertain and dangerous.
touch
It was ________________________________ during the final 2,000 m of the climbers' descent.

8. Judith finally persuaded her husband to fly to the Bahamas on vacation instead of to Norway.
talked
Judith finally ________________________________ to the Bahamas on vacation instead of to Norway.

9. Margaret was very disappointed that none of her teammates would defend her during the negotiation process.
stand
Margaret was very disappointed that none of her teammates would ________________________________ during the negotiation process.

10. I didn't really understand the hurtfulness of his comments until I got home.
sink
Not until I got home ________________________________ in.

ULTIMATE CHALLENGE

PART D

Sentence Reconstruction

Reconstruct the following ten sentences by putting the individual words back into their correct order. All of the sentences represent TRUE statements that can be inferred from the information presented in the reading text. Supply appropriate punctuation as needed.

1. by ever the machine is most CERN's hands complex created human LHC

___

___

___

2. the the to to into that just being moments conditions was came existed create universe those designed after similar LHC

___

___

___

3. a to at a of phenomenon than implies given principle certainty chance some sigma work causative level effect other is that five

___

___

___

4. of the as in are materials recycled many residential such using construction tires architects buildings car

___

___

___

5. of to the the the is that dizzying design sky heights and limit under skyscrapers continue assumption taller architects working taller

___

___

___

6. to of an are strong because Japan's ability engineering pagodas marvel earthquakes their withstand innate

7. of to in the on one top simply are are but storeys individual another not placed connected pagodas other rather physically each

8. an from the the the the the that to occur resulting disperse design earthquake shifts building floors energy during pagoda lateral permit staggered in

9. of to the on that and speed engineering sophisticated high architects civil structures design computers engineers test programs and rely heavily limits

10. through in of are science remarkable possible today's advances made engineering materials marvels many

LANGUAGE IN USE

PART E

I Suggested Questions for Discussion

A. What monuments or structures in your country have special historical significance? Describe these structures briefly and elaborate on their importance in your country's history.

B. Describe your own "dream home"—if money were no obstacle to its construction.

C. Many architects and urban planners have complained about a growing monotony of international style, which in many instances has replaced historically evolved, traditional styles in a number of cities around the world. Present your own observations to either support or negate this view.

II Suggested Questions for Written Research Projects

A. Considering the enormous costs of the most advanced engineering marvels such as CERN's LHC, or of a number of space agencies' missions to the moon and to Mars, argue for one of the following positions:

i) Science's quest to uncover the secrets of Nature and to explore extraterrestrial environments is simply too costly and takes away funding from much-needed infrastructure projects around the world. Such projects should be halted.

ii) The human goal to explore the expanse of our universe and the possible breakthroughs in knowledge to be gained through such exploration cannot be measured in monetary terms. It is impossible to predict the ways in which a greater understanding of our world may contribute to the survival of our planet. International collaboration and a common pool of resources should be set aside to further this goal.

B. Describe the most important engineering projects that should be funded in your country. What obstacles are involved in completing those projects, and how might these obstacles be overcome?

C. Describe and outline your own topic-related research question.

UNIT 10

GOING TO EXTREMES

BEFORE YOU READ

What's the most exciting sport you've ever participated in? Which sporting events do you prefer to watch as a spectator? Would you ever become involved in a sport that is inherently dangerous? Why or why not? Have you ever engaged in sports considered to be dangerous? If YES, what dangers were involved?

DIRECTIONS: As you read the following text, complete the blanks after the numbered brackets with an appropriate form of the word given in capital letters. The first one has been done for you as an example.

CLOZE TASK

A Many people around the world, but especially young men in their twenties, seem to have a death wish. Not content to challenge fate by merely sitting at the edge of a cliff hundreds of meters above the ground, the daredevils of extreme sports push themselves to the limits of what is physically, [0] HUMAN humanly possible.

B The most extreme of these modern-era "sports" (if they can even truly be called such), are what one might describe as one-off situations for the [1] PARTICIPATE______________________. Put somewhat more crudely, the person actively engaged in the death-defying endeavors of extreme sports either completes the impossible mission successfully, or most likely ends up six feet under.

C Testing the limits of both skill and [2] ENDURE _______________, free climbers seem somehow convinced that they have landed real-life roles as spidermen as they scale the sheer sides of mountains and cliffs without any traditional equipment, such as picks or ropes. At each stage of the climb, they rely on nothing but the strength of their own muscles to hold their fingertips daintily inside the cracks of rock surfaces with their toes perched on precarious ledges of mere centimeters in width. One wrong move or the sudden [3] CRUMB ______________________ of a precipice thought to have been solid, and the climbers would plummet to their deaths.

Image production credit: iStock.com/ gregepperson

D One master free-climber, Alex Honnold, set a number of records for fastest solo free climbs, chief among these being the 5-hour, 49-minute ascent of the 900 meter Nose of El Capitan in California's Yosemite Valley. It should be noted that this particular spot is especially treacherous because the angle of ascent is nearly vertical. At one point in the ascent, [4] CLIMB______________________ must cling to the underside of an outcropping with their backs to the ground!

E Only slightly less dangerous but equally [5] SPECTACLE ______________________ is wingsuit skydiving. Even the normal, more established forms of skydiving involve potential danger as both a parachute and its backup can fail to open. Members of skydiving teams have also fallen to their deaths when their cords have become [6] TANGLE

______________________. But those who challenge nature's most relentless force have managed to take the exhilaration gained from merely jumping out of an airplane to a new level of [7] EXCITE ____________. Once in free-fall mode, these would-be human birds spread the wings of their bat-like bodysuits and allow the synthetic webbing between their legs and under their arms to create enough drag to let the airborne thrill-seekers glide over impressive distances. Shin Ito of Japan managed to glide 23.1 km after a jump from 9,800 meters. For every meter that gravity brings them closer to earth, wingsuit skydivers are able to fly 2.5 meters forward.

F In addition to the wingsuit worn by the flyer, a parachute is also carried on the back for [8] DEPLOY____________________ at a chosen altitude. Most countries require wingsuit jumpers to have completed a minimum of 200 skydives with a traditional parachute prior to attempting a wingsuit flight.

Image production credit: iStock.com/ Cisquete

G Of course, experts in the art quickly became involved in even more elaborately breathtaking challenges, such as flying within inches of the sheer sides of cliffs, rocketing through the undersides of bridges, and even leaping from the tops of buildings such as Chicago's Sears Tower for a unique bird's-eye tour between skyscrapers, as seen in the film *Transformers: Dark of the Moon.*

H Widely regarded as the most dangerous of all extreme sports, underwater spelunking, also known as cave diving, has tallied up a tragic list of [9] FATAL____________________ over the years to support its honorary title. A number of the world's underwater cave systems, such as those in north-central Florida and the blue hole systems in the Bahamas, are [10] ENTICE____________________ beautiful labyrinths containing tunnel systems in complete darkness.

Without a proper fail-safe guide line anchored to the exit into open water, divers can simply lose their way and [11] MISTAKE ___________ wander off even farther into the maze of tunnels. Once the [12] REALIZE____________________ sets in that they've taken a wrong turn somewhere, panic may cause the divers to [13] BREATH __________ much more rapidly, thus depleting their already limited supply of precious oxygen. Lights with [14] RELY ____________________ backups are also critical in such difficult surroundings. Occasionally, the swimming motion of the divers can stir up silt deposits from the bottom of the caverns, reducing [15] VISIBLE ____________________ to zero. Cave walls and other interior structures may also give way, perhaps blocking the only exit back to the surface. In addition, many underwater cave systems are fraught with strong inflow and outflow currents. Trapped in an intense inflow current, divers might easily be [16] POWER____________________ by the force of the water, carrying them farther and farther away from the exit hole with little hope of [17] SURVIVE____________________ in this dark, claustrophobic world without air.

Image production credit: iStock.com/ifish

J Unlike normal open ocean descents into the deep, plunges into the alien world of cave systems usually involve [18] CONSIDER __________ distances traversed [19] HORIZON ______________ well beneath the surface. If something should go tragically wrong, divers would first have to reverse and make their way all the way back horizontally before they could even begin their ascent back to the surface. The swim back up must also be accomplished [20] PATIENCE ____________________ and with extreme care so that a potential buildup of nitrogen bubbles in the diver's blood doesn't lead to "the bends," an often fatal condition.

K Divers who have been investigating the earth's most mysterious underwater caverns over the years have come up with a mnemonic warning: **T**he **G**ood **D**ivers **A**re **L**iving. The initial letter in each word of the warning refers to the cardinal safety measures that must be in place before anyone ever attempts cave diving. The "T" stands for the extensive training program that must be successfully completed. "G" refers to that life-saving guide line that must be secured in two separate places near the surface and near the entrance to the cave. "D" is for depth management, meaning that divers must at all times be acutely aware of how far they are descending. The allowable depth of a dive is highly dependent on the type of breathing apparatus and on the air ("A") or gas mixture used. More critical types of cave dives to greater depths rely on expensive "rebreather" equipment systems that effectively [21] CIRCLE_________________ the carbon dioxide exhaled to produce breathable oxygen. The final "L" stands for adequate lighting. In the pitch-black darkness of submarine caves, no light whatsoever penetrates from the surface of the water. If divers become uncoupled from their guide lines, without adequate lighting, they might end up in a panicked state, unable to reconnect or to even locate the guide line again.

L Surely more [22] PLEASURE____________________ thrills await all those water buffs who have somehow mastered the art of skimming along the surface of ocean waves balanced on a surfboard. A few locations around the world are renowned for their often ideal surfing conditions, including the southern coast of California and the North Shore of Oahu in Hawaii. Others, such as Mavericks on the northern California coast; Teahupoo in Tahiti; Peahi, which is also known as "Jaws" in Hawaii; and Hout Bay, near Cape Town, South Africa, are [23] FAME ____________________ for their treacherous surfing conditions.

M In terms of the waves themselves, bigger is not always better, but the giant walls of water do make for ideal [24] PHOTO_______________ backdrops for surfers who can tame some of the giants among ocean waves. As a general rule, the bigger the wave, the greater the potential danger involved for the surfer who "wipes out" or is thrown off her board by the force of the water. That said, when surfers do succeed in riding the ocean's giants, the results are often spectacular. In the spring of 2012, professional surfer Garrett McNamara from Hawaii broke all previous records by successfully maneuvering a wall of water 23.77 meters in [25] HIGH ______________________ near Praia do Norte off the coast of Portugal.

N As the adage puts it, records are there to be broken. In the fall of 2013, Brazilian surfer Carlos Burle rode a 100-foot wave to trump Garrett McNamara's previous record by 22 feet near the same Portuguese town of Nazare. Burle had been assisted by Nature herself as a massive storm pounded the west coast of Europe.

Image production credit: iStock.com/rhyman007

O Although out in the middle of nowhere, one particularly interesting region for surfers is known as the Cortes Bank, situated approximately 160 km off the coast of San Diego, California. Because of an underwater mountain chain that rises to within a meter or two just beneath the surface, waves often form here under "ideal conditions" and are capable of reaching heights in excess of 30 meters. The main problem is that the region is so remote that would-be surfers must be flown in by helicopter or small plane and then dropped into position.

P Over the years, a number of even expert surfers have succumbed to the ocean's power. To understand why, just do the math. One liter of water weighs one kilogram. When a 15-meter wave crashes down on a surfer from above, the enormous weight of the water directly above forces the surfer's body into the depths of water below, that is, if she's lucky. In many areas known for their challenging conditions, sharp coral reefs or jagged boulders may lie just a few meters beneath the surface, causing serious lacerations, broken bones, and concussions that can render the surfer unconscious. Even if there are no obstacles below, the surfer who is thrown to the depths by the force of the crushing waves can easily become [26] ORIENT__________________ and unable to recognize which way is up. If a second or third wave then hits in rapid succession, the surfer might be completely overcome by the water and simply drown. The so-called "Pipeline" on Oahu's famous North Shore reportedly claims the record for causing the greatest number of fatalities among surfers for these very reasons.

Q Considering the perils inherent in extreme forms of sport such as the ones described, one has to wonder why on earth sane human beings would ever opt to put their lives at risk by engaging in such activities, knowing full well what the possible outcome might be. Recent studies (Bardo, Williams, Dwoskin, Moynahan, Perry & Martin, 2007) of the brain functions of extreme sports enthusiasts have shown that thrill seekers who will go to virtually any length to obtain the "high" brought on in the chasm between life and death display lower levels of monamine oxidase activity. In addition, the neurological expression of dopamine [27] RECEIVE ______________________ and dopamine transporters appears to be altered.

As Bardo et al. point out, reduced monoamine function has also been implicated in a variety of psychiatric disorders, leading researchers to posit a clear link between various types of addiction, death-defying thrill seeking, and abnormal neurological brain [28] CHEMIST____________________.

R As already noted, extreme sports of various types are most frequently the domain of young men in their late adolescent years or early adulthood. Numerous studies (Blakemore & Choudhury, 2006; Caseya, Tottenhama, Listona & Durstona, 2005; Dahl, 2004; Steinberg, 2007) have shown that the dorsal lateral prefrontal cortex, which is critical in the control of impulses, does not reach maturity until later. Psychiatrists and psychologists have most frequently attempted to address problematic behavior in adolescents and young adults through counseling in close collaboration with the parents of the individuals involved. These neurological findings would seem to indicate that teens in particular are not merely "acting out" as a result of a propensity toward bad behavior, but rather that they are not yet fully equipped with the necessary hardwiring that would allow them to thoroughly assess risks and dangers, and to act appropriately in the face of danger. Such insights from neuroscience will pave the way for more effective therapeutic regimens to treat cases of uncontrolled behavior that might [29] DANGER____________________ the person in question or his/her surroundings.

S The mere appearance of extreme sports as just a more intense version of the more mundane varieties of athletic activity makes it exceedingly difficult to draw a distinct line between what is truly "insane" in its death-defying nature, and what is an acceptable norm. Quite often, those who would push the limits of what is normal have found themselves forced to rely on rescue teams who are then put into action to pull the individual(s) to [30] SAFE____________________, often at enormous financial costs to the community responsible for the rescue. When these same daredevils are then forced to cough up the hundreds of thousands of dollars to pay for the rescue, they may start to think twice before embarking on an impossible mission.

REFERENCES

Bardo, M. T., Williams, Y., Dwoskin, L. P., Moynaham, S. E., Perry, I. B. & Martin, C. A. (2007). The sensation seeking trait and substance use: Research findings and clinical implications. *Current Psychiatry Reviews*, *3*, 3–13. doi: 10.1196/annals.1308.009

Blakemore, S.-J. & Choudhury, S. (2006, March/April). Development of the adolescent brain: Implications for executive function and social cognition. *Journal of Child Psychology and Psychiatry*, *47*(3–4), 296–312. doi: 10.1111/j.1469-7610.2006.01611.x

Caseya, B. J., Tottenhama, N., Listona, C. & Durstona, S. (2005, March 1). Imaging the developing brain: What have we learned about cognitive development? *Trends in Cognitive Sciences*, *9*(3), 104–110. doi: 10.1016/j.tics.2005.01.011

Dahl, R. (2004). Adolescent brain development: A period of vulnerabilities and opportunities. *Annals of the New York Academy of Sciences, 1021,* 1 - 22.

Steinberg, L. (2007, April). Risk taking in adolescence. New perspectives from brain and behavioral science. *Current Directions in Psychological Science*, *16*(2), 55–59. doi: 10.1111/j.1467-8721.2007.00475.x

POST-READING QUESTIONS

1. What new information did you learn from reading the text?
2. What facts or figures surprised you when reading the text?
3. Which of the described extreme sports made you think you might like to try it? Why?
4. Which of the described extreme sports made you feel jittery when reading about it?
5. Why is cave diving considered the most dangerous extreme sport?
6. Describe the influence of brain development on an individual's perceptions of danger.
7. Explain how wingsuit skydiving works.
8. In your own words, explain the phrase "The Good Divers Are Living."

VOCABULARY WORK

PART A

From the reading text, find the words or phrases that have similar meanings to the words / phrases given in the numbered lists below. The first one has been done for you as an example.

From Paragraphs A–J:	Synonymous Word or Phrase
1. to climb	scale (paragraph C)
2. a drop-off; precipice	__________
3. entail; include	__________
4. delicately; artistically	__________
5. fearless, intrepid adventurers	__________
6. in the grave; dead	__________
7. ventures; adventures; undertakings	__________
8. iffy; uncertain; unsure; shaky; unsecured	__________
9. reserve; extra supply; replacement	__________
10. dangerous; perilous	__________
11. protrusion; overhang	__________
12. cliff; bluff	__________
13. merriment; glee; alacrity; elan	__________
14. plunge; nosedive	__________
15. unswerving; unyielding; inexorable	__________
16. before; in advance of	__________
17. elevation	__________
18. mesh; interlacement; tight latticework	__________
19. resistance; the pull exerted on a wing to reduce downward motion	__________
20. mazes	__________
21. caves; grottos	__________

22. jumping ______________________
23. exploring caves ______________________
24. having a strong fear of closed, tight spaces ______________________
25. (noun) dives; drops ______________________
26. lethal; deadly ______________________
27. climb; upward movement ______________________
28. rapid dive into the depths ______________________

From Paragraphs K–S: Synonymous Word or Phrase

29. anchored; fastened ______________________
30. related to memory; helping the memory ______________________
31. of principal or prime importance ______________________
32. far away; isolated ______________________
33. handling; manipulating; navigating ______________________
34. died as a result of; capitulated to ______________________
35. changed ______________________
36. split; cleft ______________________
37. inclination; tendency; proneness ______________________
38. courses of medical treatment or therapy ______________________
39. deaths ______________________
40. commencing; undertaking; venturing into; setting out on ______________________
41. to contribute to or give to reluctantly ______________________

VOCABULARY WORK

PART B

Choose an appropriate form of one of the words given below to complete the numbered sentences that follow. Two of the words have been used twice.

ALTER	LIFT
ALTITUDE	MANEUVER
BACKUP	PLUMMET
CARDINAL	PRIOR TO
CLAUSTROPHOBIA	PROPENSITY
EMBARK	REMOTE
ENDEAVOR	SECURE

1. At many companies and research institutes, employees are required to ____________ their work into the company's external or cloud storage.

2. The ____________________ rule of many fast-paced ball sports is this: keep your eye on the ball!

3. Helicopters, which routinely move forward and backward as well as up and down in rapid succession, achieve greater ____________________ over conventional airplanes, but they also place greater demands on the flying skills of those who pilot them.

4. During the earliest years of European immigration to America, most of those who ____________________ on the long journey by sea realized it was a one-way trip.

5. Cars with mid-position placement of the engine and rear-wheel drive are generally much more ____________________ than are other types of vehicles, which explains why this is the standard for Formula 1 vehicles.

6. International space exploration has never ____________________ to send humans on the long voyage to Mars, though various plans to do so have been on the drawing boards for some time.

7. Airplanes of a blended wing design achieve much greater __________ with significantly less power required, resulting in enormous fuel savings and greater overall stability.

ALTER	LIFT
ALTITUDE	MANEUVER
BACKUP	PLUMMET
CARDINAL	PRIOR TO
CLAUSTROPHOBIA	PROPENSITY
EMBARK	REMOTE
ENDEAVOR	SECURE

8. When the horizontal stabilizer breaks or is rendered inoperable on an airplane, the craft ________________________ straight to the ground in a nosedive position.

9. Minor clothing ________________________, such as hemming the legs of trousers or letting out / taking in a few centimeters in the waist, do not require expert-level tailoring skills.

10. Light from the ________________________ objects in the visible universe requires more than 13 billion years to reach us.

11. Specialists in human resources have repeatedly said that most job applicants get rejected simply because the candidates have failed to thoroughly research the company or institute ________________________ submitting their application package.

12. Although most snakes have a ________________________ to shy away from humans, both the Black Mamba of sub-Saharan Africa and the feared Taipan of Australia have actually been known to chase humans.

13. Many people refuse to conduct banking transactions online out of ________________________ concerns.

14. For someone who is severely ________________________, the thought of being locked inside a closet would almost be as bad as being buried alive.

15. Transcontinental flights usually cruise at an ________________________ of approximately 10,000 meters.

16. All professional tennis players carry several ________________________ racquets just in case a string breaks.

LANGUAGE FOCUS

PART C

1. What is the implied meaning of the phrase "nature's most relentless force" in paragraph E?

2. What is the implied meaning of the phrase "six feet under" in paragraph B?

3. In paragraphs A–C, identify two reduced relative clauses that have been placed pre-positional to the noun subjects they modify.

4. Identify two types of conditionals found in paragraph P.

5. What phrase could replace the term "fail-safe" in the first sentence of paragraph I ("Without a proper fail-safe guide line anchored to the exit …")? What (if any) sentence modifications would need to be made to the original sentence if your suggested substitute phrase were used?

Sentence Transformation

For questions 6–10, use the word given below the first sentence to complete the second sentence in the blanks provided. Use between three and eight words including the given word. The given word must NOT be changed in any way, and the meaning of the sentences should be as similar as possible.

Example: We eagerly await a renewed encounter with you in the future.
forward
We are really looking forward to seeing you again in the future.

6. You're going to be signing away your freedom if you agree to the terms of this contract.
up
Agreeing to the terms of this contract will essentially mean ____________ ____ freedom.

7. The house is worth much more, so don't accept less than 50% more of all the standing offers.
settle
The house is worth much more, so ______________________________ than 50% more of all the standing offers.

8. I'm not able to answer questions of this nature so let me connect you to someone who can.

   put

   I'm not able to answer questions of this nature so let me ______________ ____ someone who can.

9. Charlotte and James gave their daughter the name of Scotland's first queen.

   after

   Charlotte and James ____ Scotland's first queen.

10. It's awful that the children were making jokes about the new boy's old clothes.

    fun

    It's awful that the children were __________________________________ the new boy's old clothes.

PART D

Sentence Reconstruction

ULTIMATE CHALLENGE

Reconstruct the following ten sentences by putting the individual words back into their correct order. All of the sentences represent TRUE statements that can be inferred from the information presented in the reading text. Supply appropriate punctuation as needed.

1. any as or or aids challenge customary scaling picks sides climbers climbing fate such without by ropes the free rocks mountains of

   ____

   ____

   ____

2. their their of the to a phases stop jumpers fall descent on last parachute wingsuit during traditional rely

   ____

   ____

   ____

3. in of the is most diving dangerous cave total fatalities extreme sport terms

___

___

___

4. of in the maze can diving complex because cave tunnels is underwater become especially divers dangerous lost easily

___

___

___

5. in to of and may who may which their rapid become oxygen turn panic divers supply breathing disoriented depletion lead faster

___

___

___

6. the the the the a a to to for cave line entrance breathing securely cave valuable fastened is divers most near equipment position piece guide besides of apparatus

___

___

___

7. the the of to too in buildup who quickly a bubbles ascend bloodstream risk nitrogen divers surface dying from

___

___

___

8. in that sharp surfing feature coastal large coral is areas waves particularly reefs dangerous

____

____

____

9. of of the the in in for sports a maturity balanced full extreme assessment brain involved required areas is critical dangers

____

____

____

10. in in to who themselves extreme teams conditions enthusiasts called community adverse rescue search trapped sports funded are find often

____

____

____

PART E

LANGUAGE IN USE

I Suggested Questions for Discussion

A. Would you ever marry someone who was passionately engaged in an extreme sport? Why?

B. In your view, what type of personality is motivated to risk life and limb in an extreme sport?

C. Of all the extreme sports you've heard about, which would you find the most appealing, and which would you never consider under any circumstances?

II Suggested Questions for Written Research Projects

A. Extreme sport—but occasionally even more established athletic events—often end in tragedy for the individuals involved and for their families. In many instances, community-based rescue operations are deployed at substantial costs to taxpayers. In light of these dangers and the ensuing financial burden on the families and communities, should governments regulate the types of sports individuals should be allowed to participate in? Or rather, should individuals be free to test the limits of their abilities irrespective of the dangers involved?

   Present a cogent argument for one or the other position.

B. Several research studies have cited a link between the addictive brain and that of the individual who derives a "rush" or a thrill from participating in extremely dangerous sports. Write a summary report assessing the most current available research findings on this link.

C. Describe and outline your own topic-related research question.

NATURE'S AWESOME POWER AND LINGERING SECRETS

UNIT 11

BEFORE YOU READ

Have you ever seen or experienced the power of nature firsthand? What happened and how did you react?

CLOZE TASK

DIRECTIONS: As you read the following text, fill in the numbered blanks with ONE suitable word.

A It almost seems that every now and then nature decides to [1]__________________ us a few lessons we'll never forget. Natural disasters often [2]__________________ without warning, wiping entire communities off the map and killing tens or even hundreds of thousands. When calamities occur, we can do little [3]__________________ but donate to relief efforts as we sit passively, almost helplessly, by as nature [4]__________________ its course.

B Many people who've experienced earthquakes, hurricanes, and tornadoes don't hesitate to award tornadoes the highest marks for the utter terror experienced during the event. Now measured on the "Enhanced Fujita" scale (Fujita, 1971), tornadoes are nature's most violent storms. F5 tornadoes, which happen to be the strongest and, fortunately, also the rarest, have been known to attain widths at ground level of 3 km and to generate winds in excess of 500 km per hour. At those speeds, tornadoes are [5]__________________ of inflicting all the damage an earthquake can do and more, albeit on a much narrower path. Even the most mundane items like soda straws, pieces of cardboard, or a toothbrush can become deadly projectiles that sever limbs or penetrate vital organs. Flying refrigerators, trucks, or freight trains become, quite literally, weapons of mass destruction.

C Tornadoes form most often at the convergence zones of colliding air masses. These types of collisions are particularly common in "tornado alley" in the center of the United States. Owing to the special geographic features of the [6]______________________, cool, dry air masses from west of the Rocky Mountains often sweep in over warm, moist air masses that have settled into the area from the Gulf of Mexico. The cold air may fall at a rapid speed as the warm air rises in the same location, often [7]______________________ rise to counterclockwise rotation.

D Fortunately for areas often hit by tornadoes, the widespread use of Doppler radar (May, Biggerstaff & Xue, 2007; Wood & Brown, 1997) has enabled storm watchers at key weather tracking stations to closely [8]______________________ storm activity for the telltale indicator of tornado formation: a counterclockwise "hook" shape at the leading edge of a storm system, signaling air rotation and the formation of a potentially deadly vortex. Alarms then sound and alerts go out, giving residents in the best-case scenario a few, often critical life-saving minutes to take [9] ______________________.

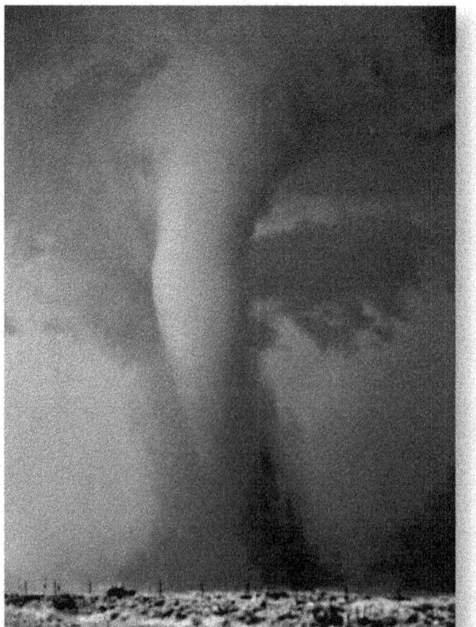

Image production credit: iStock.com/stormchase

E In sharp contrast to menacing storms that visibly warn us of impending danger, the earth beneath our feet seems to be the safest, most reliable, and most predictable feature of our planet. But here, too, nature holds many surprises in store. Generated by the sudden shifting of intersecting tectonic plates deep beneath the earth's surface along fault zones, earthquakes strike completely without warning. Most frequently gauged or measured on the logarithmic open-ended Richter scale, earthquake magnitudes can range from completely imperceptible levels of 1 or 2 to events releasing thousands of times the energy produced by the Hiroshima atomic bomb—the higher the magnitude, the greater the devastation. The two most common types of tectonic plate collision involve either thrust faults, on which an oceanic plate—such as the massive Pacific Plate—moves beneath a continental plate, or strike-slip faults, along which two giant plate masses slide horizontally next to each other. The most powerful earthquake ever [10]____________, a magnitude 9.5 off the coast of Chile in 1960, occurred along an oceanic subduction zone (thrust fault), where for eons the Nazca Plate has been sliding eastward under the South America Plate, producing the Andes Mountains in the process (Chlieh et al., 2004). Forty-four years later on December 26, 2004, a megathrust submarine fault off the west coast of Sumatra slipped suddenly and violently. The quake measured between 9.1 and 9.3 and lasted just under ten minutes—the longest of any known seismic event. The violent upheaval produced a massive tsunami that reached heights of up to 30 m and killed nearly a quarter of a million people in 13 countries flanking the Indian Ocean and Andaman Sea. Millions were left homeless as the giant waves wiped entire communities off the map.

F In March of 2011, another 9.0 megathrust quake occurred 32 km beneath the Pacific approximately 70 km off the eastern coast of Japan. The Pacific Plate, which is the largest of earth's tectonic structures, suddenly pushed westward, subducting under the Eurasian Plate and pushing the entire island of Honshu eastward toward North America by more than two meters. According to GPS data, the quake was [11]__________________ powerful that the entire earth shifted on its axis by more than 10 cm.

Within minutes, tsunamis of up to 40 m pounded the Japanese coast, killing thousands, destroying virtually the entire infrastructure of the region, and knocking out critical facilities at the Fukushima nuclear power plant. Radioactivity in the form of Caesium 137, released by the explosions and subsequent meltdown of the cores, threatens to make vast swaths of land [12]__________________ for decades to come and to destroy much of the marine life in that region of the Pacific. Fears quickly mounted that even more radioactivity would be released into the entire northern hemisphere if reactor number four suffered additional damage through subsequent tremors.

G The second type of earthquake occurs along strike-slip fault zones. Activity along California's San Andreas fault represents this type of tectonic movement. In the southern region of California, the key cities of Los Angeles, San Diego, and Santa Barbara lie on the easternmost edge of the Pacific Plate and are moving north-northwest, whereas San Francisco and all other areas of the continent are [13]______________________ south-southeast on the North America Plate. Over the millennia, the two plates will continue to move past each other so that eventually Los Angeles and San Francisco might theoretically be next-door neighbors.

H It is important to remember that earthquakes themselves do not kill; buildings do. In all areas of the west coast of the United States, a seismically highly active region, strict building codes force engineers, architects, and contractors to use as many established safety procedures and reinforcement devices as are economically feasible so that key [14]__________________ structures such as hospitals, government buildings, and schools can [15]______________________ the shockwaves generated by major quakes. Designed with the foreknowledge that earthquakes are going to occur, the tallest, most modern buildings in Tokyo are [16]_____________ with any number of elaborate systems to minimize the damage that might potentially result from the p (primary) and s (secondary) waves. Some of these structures incorporate base isolation systems that separate the foundation from the superstructure and thus [17]____________________ the impact of the waves before they hit the upper floors of the buildings themselves. Others employ counterbalance designs that offset the swaying with counter-motion. The same types of elaborate systems can also be found in Taipei 101, the tallest building in seismically active Taiwan.

I But in view of the scale and magnitude of destruction, one other type of natural [18]____________________ has had what can only be described as a cataclysmic impact on earth's geological and biological history (Miller & Wark, 2008). As devastating as earthquakes and nature's most violent storms have been and are, these forces pale in [19] ____________________ to the truly catastrophic damage unleashed by super-volcanoes. Over the last 25 million years in earth's geological history, the explosion of Lake Toba on the Indonesian island of Sumatra 75,000 years ago ranks as the sole "mega-colossal" eruption. According to well-researched estimates, the explosion at Lake Toba sent the unfathomable volume of 2,800 km^3 of debris into the atmosphere, along with six billion tons of sulfur dioxide and 10 billion tons of sulfuric acid. The effects on the environment would have been unimaginable as thick layers of ash covered all of southern Asia, while ash clouds darkened the skies for years, [20]____________________ out sunlight—which is critical for plant and animal survival along the entire food chain—and sending temperatures into the basement.

Image production credit: iStock.com/tjuktjuk

J The threat of super-volcanic eruptions is by no means the sole prerogative of ancient history. Yellowstone National Park (James, Fouch,

Carlson & Roth, 2011; Kelbert, Egbert & deGroot-Hedlin, 2012; Leeman, Schutt & Hughes, 2009; Lowenstern & Hurwitz, 2008; Pierce & Morgan, 2009) in North America is long overdue for another colossal explosion. The massive caldera, which covers practically the entire area of the national park, produces super-volcanic eruptions approximately every 600,000 years, and the last mega-eruption was 620,000 years ago. A number of geologists cite rates of super-eruptions [21]____________________ on earth at least once every 100,000 years, and according to Stephen Sparks of the University of Bristol, that [22]____________________ might even be closer to once every 50,000 years.

K An eruption at Yellowstone would make life in many parts of the United States simply impossible. Farms, forests, rivers, and streams would be unable to support any forms of life, as thick layers of ash would [23]____________________ everything in sight, smothering people, animals, and all forms of vegetation.

L As much as we might fear or dread nature's nasty surprises, as a never-ending enigma she is also an awe-inspiring source of immense wonderment. The earth's entire history, and indeed that of our solar system, is but a brief [24]____________________ in time against a backdrop of the conceptually infinite. Through the wonders of modern engineering, the tools [25]____________________ which we can observe the farthest reaches of the visible universe have made possible measurements and theories previous generations could not even have imagined. X-ray and infrared telescopes and the Hubble optical telescope have allowed us glimpses of galaxies and clusters of galaxies whose primordial framework resulted from slightly uneven distributions of matter and energy shortly after the Big Bang.

M But there is something about the universe that just doesn't make sense; the numbers simply don't [26]____________________ up. Astronomer Fritz Zwicky from the California Institute of Technology first noticed the problem back in 1933 while conducting an extensive survey of the Coma cluster, a group of approximately 1,000 galaxies. Zwicky observed that at the speeds at which the individual galaxies were moving within the cluster, the entire group should have been torn apart. Since this was not the [27]____________________, Zwicky reasoned that something other than the observed masses of galaxies must be keeping the cluster intact. In 1976, astrophysicist Vera Rubin was studying the movement patterns of spiral galaxies, a fairly common shape found in galaxies like our own Milky Way and the Andromeda galaxy, our nearest neighbor. Extensive calculations (Rubin, 1998) have shown quite clearly that the stars within these galaxies are moving much faster than the force of gravity, as calculated based solely on the observed mass within the galaxies should allow. In other words, here, [28]____________________, something unknown to astronomy and physics was keeping both the galaxies and observed clusters of galaxies intact. Inexplicably, a full 85% of all the gravity associated with our universe is simply unaccounted [29]______________. Zwicky referred to the problem as missing matter; today, the enigma goes by the name *dark matter*.

N A great deal of speculation and experimental research today (Ahmed et al., 2010; Bertonea, Hooper & Silk, 2004) is focused on possible candidates for dark matter, such as Weakly Interacting Massive Particles (WIMPS)—a posited unknown species of particle that has yet to be identified. [30]____________________ constitutes dark matter does not have any of the characteristics associated with normal forms of matter, including any conventional form of interaction, except of course through the exertion of gravitational force. It has even been suggested that perhaps our fundamental concepts of gravity are wrong, necessitating a complete modification of Newtonian dynamics—a line of thought now identified by the acronym MOND. [31]____________________ line of thought has proposed that the gravitational force holding our galaxies together is the result of ordinary matter contained in a parallel universe that might exist right next to ours, and that gravity waves are constantly being leaked between these parallel universes.

O To make matters even worse in terms of all that we simply don't know about our universe—with repeated measurements using references such as globular clusters of old stars in the centers of galaxies, Cepheid variables, and class 1a supernovae (Riess et al., 2007)—a great number of studies show that the light reaching us today from the farthest known, and hence most ancient galaxies, is highly red-shifted, confirming that some strange "dark force" is causing the universe to expand at a highly accelerated rate inexplicable within our current models in physics and cosmology. In fact, the galaxies that are farthest apart within our visible universe are now receding away from each other faster than the speed of light. This does not imply that the objects themselves are actually moving faster than the speed of light, but that space itself is inflating so rapidly that all objects "contained" in it are in effect receding from each other at such breakneck speed—much like ink points drawn on a balloon suddenly recede from each other when the balloon is blown up very quickly. As the most distant galaxies move farther and faster away from us, the light they [32]______________________ will no longer be able to reach our regions of the universe. These billions of galaxies will eventually disappear past our existence horizon, and thus be forever lost beyond the fabric of our own realm of space-time. [33]______________________ we now detect is the last glimmer of light that we will ever see from them. (For a lucid explanation of this strange phenomenon, see Cornell University's astronomy discussion at: http://curious.astro.cornell.edu/question.php?number=575 and the clarifications of relativity and the accelerated expansion of the universe at: http://www.astro.ucla.edu/~wright/cosmology_faq.html#FTL.)

P Previous conjecture had asked [34]______________________ there might be enough mass in the known universe to allow gravity not only to slow down the hyper-inflationary expansion that kicked in at some point after the Big Bang, but also to pull everything back into a type of cosmic singularity in one gigantic "crunch." Today we know that this will not be the case. Instead, all star systems will eventually be so far removed from each other through the accelerating [35] ______________________ that any survivors on our planet or other solar systems would see nothing but a black sky, completely devoid of any [36]______________________.

Q In July of 2012, a team of physicists from the University of

Michigan at Ann Arbor announced that actual direct observations of dark matter had been made between galaxy clusters Abell 222 and Abell 223 (Dietrich et al., 2012). This was the first-ever direct sighting of dark matter, but seeing and detecting are one thing; actually understanding the makeup of dark matter is something quite different. Today, theoretical physicists and astrophysicists continue to rack their brains [37]__________________ to figure out just what the nature of both "dark matter" and the even more mysterious "dark energy" might be. In a word, we are essentially clueless as to what dark energy and dark matter are, but they are enormously important for our understanding of the nature of the universe. After all, the generally accepted breakdown today of all that is known to exist in the universe leaves the visible world we see around us pretty much holding the short end of the stick: roughly 68% dark energy; 27% dark matter; and 5% visible or "normal" matter.

R To complicate things even further, cosmological observations and measurements conducted in 1986–1987 by a group of astronomers [38]________________________ as the "Seven Samurai" confirmed that some unknown "Great Attractor" is pulling our own Milky Way, our nearest neighbor, the Andromeda Galaxy, our entire "Local Group" of galaxies, and the entire Virgo Cluster of galaxies into it at a truly astronomical speed. The Great Attractor itself lies a "mere" 250 million light years from our own galaxy, but the force of its [39]__________________ cannot be explained with conventional theories of gravity alone. Beyond the Great Attractor at a distance of approximately 650 million light years from the Milky Way lies the largest known matter-dense structure in the local universe, the Shapley Supercluster. A study (Proust, Quintana, Carrasco, Reisenegger, Slezak, Muriel, et al.) conducted in 2006 confirmed that "this mass would represent only half of that required to attract the Local Group in the direction of the supercluster."

S What is, then, responsible for the enormous pull being [40] ________________________ on the thousands of galaxies in our vicinity, including our own Milky Way? What strange, unknown force can explain the unfathomable speed with which the universe is expanding? What unseen mass of matter is binding the visible universe into filaments, megastructures in a grand cosmic web?

T We have not been able to reconcile our repeated observations with existing models of gravity, mass, and energy. Theoretical physicists continue to struggle with finding that one single magic equation—that "unified field theory"—that could finally bring together the two fundamental edifices of modern physics: Einstein's theory of relativity, and quantum mechanics. Relativity's equations and predictions not only describe most exquisitely the interrelation of matter and energy, but also guide our fundamental understanding of the fabric of space-time. At the other end of the spectrum, quantum physics holds a unique status in the history of human thought as the single most successful theory ever developed. In the quest to unite these two as yet irreconcilable pillars of physics, a number of theorists have gone back to the drawing board to re-conceive our most trusted and fundamental notions of space, time, and matter. Arguably the most progressive and courageous of scientific minds, theoretical physicists have always dared to think the unthinkable, to overturn conventional wisdom when their equations compelled them to, and to imagine the unimaginable. The hypothesized models of string theory and brane theory do just that. Thinkers as notable as David Bohm (2002) and Leonard Susskind (2006) have even argued that, just perhaps, the entire universe is essentially a holographic projection, reaching us from the horizon of our visible universe. Building on the many-worlds interpretation of quantum mechanics as first formulated by Hugh Everett (1957), thinkers such as David Deutsch (2002) see theoretical evidence for the possible existence of an entire multitude of universes (Carr, 2007; Garriga & Vilenkin, 2009), some with physical laws similar to those that govern our own cosmos, others with perhaps entirely different forces governing nature. At present, there is essentially no practical way these theoretical constructs can be tested. Nevertheless, the quest to fathom the depths of reality in all its bizarre forms continues as an obsession for all those afflicted with the insatiable desire to know.

REFERENCES

Ahmed, Z., Akerib, D. S., Arrenberg, S., Bailey, C. N., Balakishiyeva, D., Baudis, L., et al. (2010). Dark matter search results from the CDMS II experiment. *Science, 327*(5973), 1619–2010.

Bertonea, G., Hooper, D. & Silk, J. (2004, November 5). Particle darkmatter: Evidence, candidates and constraints. http://dx.doi.org/10.1016/j.physrep.2004.08.031

Bohm, D. (2002). *Wholeness and the implicate order*. London: Routledge.

Carr, B. (2007). *Universe or multiverse?* Cambridge, UK: Cambridge University Press.

Chlieh, M., de Chabalier, J. B., Ruegg, J. C., Armijo, R., Dmowska, R., Campos, J. (2004, July 14). Crustal deformation and fault slip during the seismic cycle in the North Chile subduction zone, from GPS and InSAR observations. *Geophysical Journal International, 158*(2), 695—711. doi: 10.1111/j.1365-246X.2004.02326.x

Deutsch, D. (2002). The structure of the multiverse. Proceedings of the Royal Society, London A. 8 December 2002, *458*(2028), 2911–2923.

Dietrich, J., Werner, N., Clowe, D., Finoguenov, A., Kitching, T., Miller, L., et al. (2012, July). A filament of dark matter between two clusters of galaxies. *Nature, 487*(7406), 202–204. http://dx.doi.org/10.1038/nature11224

Everett, H. (1957, July). Relative state formulation of quantum mechanics. *Reviews of Modern Physics, 29*, 454–462.

Fujita, T. (1971). Proposed characterization of tornadoes and hurricanes by area and intensity. Satellite and Mesometeorology Research Project. SMRP Research Paper Number 91. Department of the Geophysical Sciences. Chicago, IL: The University of Chicago.

Garriga, J. & Vilenkin, A. (2009, January). Holographic multiverse. *Journal of Cosmology and Astroparticle Physics*. doi: 10.1088/1475-7516/2009/01/021.

James, D. E., Fouch, M. J., Carlson, R. W. & Roth, J. B. (2011). Slab fragmentation, edge flow and the origin of the Yellowstone hotspot. *Earth and Planetary Science Letters, 311*, 124–135.

Kelbert, A., Egbert, G. D. & deGroot-Hedlin, C. (2012). Crust and upper mantle electric conductivity beneath the Yellowstone Hotspot. *Geology, 40*, 447–450. doi:10.1130/G32655.1.

Leeman, W. P., Schnutt, D. L. & Hughes, S. S. (2009). Thermal structure beneath the Snake River Plain: Implications for the Yellowstone hotspot. *Journal of Volcanology and Geothermal Research, 188*, 57–67. doi: 10.1016/j.jvolgeores.2009.01.034.

Lowenstern, J. B. & Hurwitz, S. (2008, February). Monitoring a super-volcano in repose: Heat and volatile flux at the Yellowstone Caldera. *Elements*, *4*(1), 35–40. doi: 10.2113/GSELEMENTS.4.1.35.

May, R. M., Biggerstaff, M. I. & Xue, M. (2007). A Doppler radar emulator with an application to the detectability of tornadic signatures. *Journal of Atmospheric and Oceanic Technology*, *24*(12), 1973–1996.

Miller, C. F. & Wark, D. A. (2008, February). Supervolcanoes and their explosive supereruptions. *Elements*, *4*(1), 11–15. doi: 10.2113/GSELEMENTS.4.1.11.

Pierce, K.L. & Morgan, L. A. (2009). Is the track of the Yellowstone hotspot driven by a deep mantle plume? — Review of volcanism, faulting, and uplift in light of new data. *Journal of Volcanology and Geothermal Research*. 188:1-25.

Proust, D., Quintana, H., Carrasco, E. R., Reisenegger, A., Slezak, E., Muriel, H., et al. (2006). The Shapley Supercluster: The largest matter concentration in the local universe. *The Messenger*, *124*, 30–31.

Riess, A. G., Strolger, L. G., Casertano, S., Ferguson, H. C., Bahram, M., Gold, B., et al. (2007). New Hubble space telescope discoveries of type Ia supernovae at $z \geq 1$: Narrowing constraints on the early behavior of dark energy. *The Astrophysics Journal*, *659*(1), doi: 10.1086/510378.

Rubin, V. C. (1998). Dark matter in the universe. *Scientific American Presents* (special quarterly issue: Magnificent Cosmos) *9*(1), 106–110.

Susskind, L. (2006). The cosmic landscape: String theory and the illusion of intelligent design. New York: Back Bay Books.

Wood, V. T. & Brown, R. A. (1997). Effects of radar sampling on single-Doppler velocity signatures of mesocyclones and tornadoes. *Weather Forecasting*, *12*, 928–938. http://dx.doi.org/10.1175/1520-0434(1997)012<0928:EORSOS>2.0.CO;2

POST-READING QUESTIONS

1. Which section of the text did you find most interesting and why?
2. Which facts or figures presented in the reading were completely new to you?
3. What information in the text has aroused your interest so much that you might want to read more?
4. What type of natural disaster sounds most frightening to you?
5. If it were one day possible to send humans to other planets, would you venture a trip to Mars, for example? Why?

6. Describe the difference between a strike-slip fault and a thrust fault.
7. Briefly describe the goal of a unified field theory.
8. In your own words, describe how tornadoes form.

VOCABULARY WORK

PART A

From the reading text, find the words or phrases that have similar meanings to the words / phrases given in the numbered lists below. The first one has been done for you as an example.

From Paragraphs A–J:	Synonymous Word or Phrase
1. although; in spite of the fact that; even if	albeit (paragraph B)
2. ordinary; everyday	________
3. giveaway indication; clue; revealing tip-off	________
4. funnel	________
5. verbatim; as stated; word-for-word; in the strict sense of the word	________
6. cut off; amputate	________
7. meeting together; coming together; joining; intersection	________
8. anti-clockwise	________
9. incapable of being felt, seen, heard, tasted, or smelled	________
10. indefinitely long periods of time; billions of years	________
11. the line around which a rotating body turns	________
12. incapacitating; rendering inoperable	________
13. incomprehensible	________
14. liberated; set free; let loose	________

15. desolating; demolishing; razing; destroying ______________
16. fortification; strengthening; bolstering ______________
17. use; utilize ______________
18. late; behind time; behind an expected date or time ______________
19. to quote or reference ______________
20. the large saucer-shaped basin that results from the explosion of a volcano ______________

From Paragraphs K–T: Synonymous Word or Phrase

21. puzzle; mystery ______________
22. spectacular; magnificent; eliciting a feeling of wonder and astonishment ______________
23. fleeting glances; peeks at something ______________
24. in a manner that cannot be explained ______________
25. whole; entire; unbroken; undamaged ______________
26. persons or things in contention for a role or position of some kind ______________
27. creating a need, requirement, or demand ______________
28. speculation ______________
29. lacking; wanting; sans; depleted of ______________
30. without any idea or inkling ______________
31. to resolve differences; resolve; reunite; unite ______________
32. neighborhood; nearby area ______________
33. unseat; squash; subvert ______________
34. framework; texture; cloth; structure ______________
35. fibers; threads; strands; strings ______________
36. desirous; avid; devouring ______________

37. strange; weird; abnormal; odd ____________________

38. vexed by; troubled by; struck by ____________________

PART B

VOCABULARY WORK

Choose an appropriate form of one of the words given below to complete the numbered sentences that follow. Two of the words have been used twice.

AFFLICT	MUNDANE
CANDIDATE	OVERTURN
CITE	REINFORCE
CONVERGE	SATE
DEVASTATE	TELLTALE
EMPLOY	LEASH
KNOCK OUT	VICINITY

1. The F5 tornado that struck late in the afternoon left behind scenes of total ______________________ over a 120 km^2 stretch of land.

2. Mirrorless cameras ______________________ different types of sensors from those found in digital, single-lens reflex models.

3. Surprisingly, a great many employed adults find it more difficult to cope with __________________ tasks, such as grocery shopping, cooking, and doing laundry, than to deal with professional responsibilities at work.

4. In nearly all seismically active regions of the world, concrete for use in construction needs to be ______________________ with fiber and/or steel rebar to bolster tensile strength, which is notoriously weak in concrete alone.

5. Professor Goodwine was accused of plagiarism for neglecting to ________________ key passages he had extracted from a reference source.

6. Solar storms periodically emit charges of electromagnetic radiation so intense that they are capable of ______________________ important telecommunications satellites.

AFFLICT	MUNDANE
CANDIDATE	OVERTURN
CITE	REINFORCE
CONVERGE	SATE
DEVASTATE	TELLTALE
EMPLOY	LEASH
KNOCK OUT	VICINITY

7. In the age of instant messaging, texting, and blogging, ___________ for any political office must be especially careful not to do or say anything that might quickly come back to haunt them at election time.

8. One fundamental hallmark of all academic scholarship is the proper ______________________ of referenced studies and resources.

9. Pilots often experience severe turbulence at the _________________ zones of thermally unequal air masses.

10. Individuals with chronic physical or mental ____________________, such as amyotrophic lateral sclerosis, multiple sclerosis, or Alzheimer's, frequently require long-term intensive care.

11. One consistently contentious issue dividing the left and the right in the United States centers on recurrent attempts by pro-life social conservatives to ______________________ the Supreme Court decision legalizing early-term abortions.

12. Residents living in the ______________________ of major ports complain frequently about the stench of diesel fumes coming from ships' engines.

13. A bluish discoloration of the lips and the smell of bitter almonds from the mouth are two ____________________ signs of cyanide poisoning.

14. Economically motivated migrants usually leave native countries or regions in search of ______________________ opportunities elsewhere.

15. Owners of vicious dogs are warned not to ______________________ the animals in public places such as parks or playgrounds.

16. Tiger sharks exhibit a seemingly ________________________ appetite for any blood-containing flesh.

PART C

LANGUAGE FOCUS

1. Find instances of present participles in paragraphs A–F that have been used to connect sentences in a tighter manner than would otherwise be achieved using unreduced relative clauses.

2. What verb tenses dominate in this reading passage? Why are these tenses used here?

3. Identify two instances of grammatical parallelism in paragraphs E and F.

4. Describe the semantic distinction between *farther / farthest* in paragraph O and *further* in paragraph R.

Sentence Transformation

For questions 5–10, use the word given below the first sentence to complete the second sentence in the blanks provided. Use between three and eight words including the given word. The given word must NOT be changed in any way, and the meaning of the sentences should be as similar as possible.

Example: We eagerly await a renewed encounter with you in the future.
forward
We are really looking forward to seeing you again in the future.

5. I'm sorry to say that I'm not at all attracted to camping.
appeal
I'm sorry to say that ____ at all.

6. The investigators are interpreting the man's statement as being an admission of guilt.
amounts
The investigators feel that the man's statement ____________________
____ confession.

7. The company is risking everything to get this new product developed.
   broke
   The company is ______________________________
   to get this new product developed.

8. The government is using lots of marketing tools and millions of pounds in resources to promote this national assistance program.
   ground
   To get this national assistance program ____________________,
   the government is using lots of marketing tools and millions of pounds in resources.

9. I'm sorry, but as much as I want to believe you, your explanation just doesn't add up.
   sense
   What you're saying just ______________________________,
   as much as I want to believe you.

10. These tickets are freely available to the first 20 people who fill out a request form.
    grabs
    These tickets are ______________________________
    the first 20 people who fill out a request form.

ULTIMATE CHALLENGE

PART D

Sentence Reconstruction

Reconstruct the following ten sentences by putting the individual words back into their correct order. All of the sentences represent TRUE statements that can be inferred from the information presented in the reading text. Supply appropriate punctuation as needed.

1. on the the are are scale whose measured tornadoes storms Enhanced wind violent forces most Fujita

   ____

   ____

   ____

2. of of are the total tornadoes capable category devastation nearly highest

3. air convergence of normally dissimilar zones tornadoes isothermal form masses the highly at

4. the the of when suddenly occur shift tectonic beneath earthquakes deep plates earth surface

5. or in are another one generated moving zones largest mass thrust the beneath which along is earthquakes over fault land

6. each zones slip masses horizontally two sliding fault land strike other feature past

7. of of on to the the the according is is a with amplitude logarithmic increase scale number measured every earthquakes greater Richter times magnitude shaking ten which whole temblor

8. of of the the land that along giant shifting through water floor ocean sudden are masses waves form tsunamis

____

____

____

9. out in of of an are although abundance eruptions forms that occurrence potentially events super-volcanoes infrequent life wipe cataclysmic can

____

____

____

10. of by our that that the unknown approximately completely all physicists remains perplexed universe ninety-five are constitutes fact percent

____

____

____

LANGUAGE IN USE

PART E

I Suggested Questions for Discussion

A. What are some of the mysteries of nature or scientific "hot-button" issues that interest you? Why do you find these issues engaging?

B. If you could ask, and have answered to your fullest satisfaction, two questions, what would those questions be? Why would you select those two questions?

C. What aspects of nature, of life, or of your own personal history and experience do you find most puzzling or intriguing?

II Suggested Questions for Written Research Projects

A. Write an overview of one of the most widely discussed "hot-button" issues that interests you currently.

B. Write a journalistic-style incident report about a natural event that you're familiar with.

C. Describe and outline your own topic-related research question.

UNIT 12 OUR BRAVE NEW WORLD

BEFORE YOU READ

What associations come to mind when you hear the phrase "brave new world"?

DIRECTIONS: As you read the following text, complete the blanks after the numbered brackets with an appropriate form of the word given in capital letters. The first one has been done for you as an example.

CLOZE TASK

A We humans are not masters of our [0] CREATE creations; our creations are masters of us. Transcending our ancestral [1] LINE ____________________ as hunter-gatherers, we rapidly became the planet's master toolmakers. Our neurological apparatus has equipped us with all the necessary [2] ANALYZE________________________, spatio-temporal skills to calculate complex trajectories and to use our experience in warfare to devise astonishingly accurate and [3] IMPRESS________________________ lethal nuclear, chemical, and biological weaponry capable of annihilating all forms of terrestrial life many times over—a true perversion of thought if there ever was one.

B Humans have radically, and irreversibly, altered the conditions for all forms of life on earth. Even with "the best of intentions"—when are they ever not?—we have filled the soil, air, rivers, streams, and oceans with pesticides, toxic heavy metals, carcinogenic polycyclic aromatic hydrocarbons, and long-lived radioactive nuclides. How many species have already been driven to [4] EXTINCT _____________________ as a result of instrumental reason's quest to conquer nature for short-term gains? How many more species now teeter on the cusp of non-existence as a result of both relentless, merciless slaughter and unmitigated incursion into traditional wildlife habitats by the unstoppable expansion of human settlements and industry, with no thought given to the [5] SUFFER ________________ pain being inflicted on the most vulnerable life forms. Short-term thinking and near-term profits are the hallmarks of the brief history of human development on planet Earth. Surely, what is needed is not more of the same, but a change of paradigms as we direct our focus to curb expansion and to improve our exclusive habitat in harmony with nature and with the deepest regard for its myriad life forms. Isn't it a far nobler cause to work for an environment free of poisons and perils than to acquire the latest must-have gadgetry?

C But the holistic realms of thought and emotion that we are ideally also capable of have not kept pace with our more highly evolved linear, utilitarian cognitive patterns. Empathy and mercy are often seen as the prerogatives of old-fashioned [6] RELIGION________________ thinking or of New Age enthusiasts who have somehow "lost touch with reality." Instead, we live in and are confronted with a world of banal [7] ABSTRACT________________ in a never-ending search inspired by the marketing industry for the most powerful and fastest car; the most popular, chicest hairstyle; the most impressive biceps; the highest income; and the biggest house money can buy in the most [8] EXCLUDE______________ area of residence.

D Humans have even transferred their obsessions with superlatives onto our most prized gadgets: our computers, our surrogate selves. We enjoy a remarkably ambivalent [9] RELATE____________________ with our electronic offspring and with the world of artificial intelligence looming ahead. On the one hand, we stand in awe of their sleek designs and their breathtaking ability to churn out solutions to complex problems at warp speed; on the other, many of us harbor often subconscious fears that the fruits of our [10] INVENT____________________ minds may one day become so adept at all we dream them capable of that they become our own masters, for better or for worse.

E Alan Turing's famous thought experiment, which became known as "the Turing test," [11] VISION____________________ a machine so advanced that humans might be unable to distinguish between the responses and interaction of a fellow human interlocutor and those of an elite specimen of electronic intelligence. In the minds of many, this vision has gradually drawn closer to becoming a reality as the quantity of transistors that can be engineered onto an integrated circuit has tended to double every two years, thereby positively affecting a number of key aspects of overall computer performance. This trend is now widely referred to as Moore's Law. The term itself is somewhat of a misnomer because the observed trend is [12] DESCRIBE____________________ rather than prescriptive. It is in fact one thing to observe that A becomes B with a given regularity, but quite another to posit that A must become B with the same regularity unless it can be shown that this association reflects some [13] LIE____________________ causative principle or physical law. In the case of Moore's Law, we must attribute the noteworthy and welcome increases in processing speed and capacity both to self-fulfilling [14] PROPHET____________________ and to the marvels of state-of-the-art electrical engineering, rather than to any hidden [15] CAUSE ____________________ properties inherent in the materials and production processes themselves.

F In February, 2011, U.S. TV viewers were treated to an impressive demonstration of advances in artificial intelligence as IBM's much-lauded "Watson" put the two all-time best human *Jeopardy* champions to shame. In the game, [16] CONTEST____________________ are given a fact from millions of possible choices from every conceivable arena of human knowledge. The first person to correctly formulate the question to which the given answer is the correct response receives the total dollar figure assigned to that particular answer. A sample question might look something like this:

> Answer: "Pitched in 'C,' this woodwind instrument traditionally plays the initial 'A=440' to tune the orchestra."
>
> Correct contestant's question: "What is an oboe?"

G Watson had been pre-programmed by its—should I have said "his"? —developers with tens of millions of mundane facts from every conceivable source in the English language, including common foreign words and phrases. Watson's [17] PROGRAM____________________ then set about devising algorithms that enabled the computer to compare and contrast every previously recorded answer and question in much of the game's history to select the most likely appropriate, correct question. In the process, Watson relied on "machine learning," in which correct responses are promptly integrated into the computer's already enormous database for accurate data mining. This would be [18] COMPARE________________ to a tennis player learning from every type of error she or her opponents ever made or make at any point in practice or during a match and then never making that error again under any circumstances. Watson's stellar performance during the two-day tournament earned the IBM development team the $1 million purse.

H What is rightfully frightening to many people is the prospect that an artificial super-intelligence or hybrid might eventually seek to replace us completely or might acquire a volition of its own, completely independent of any human input or control. With the human genome sequence unraveled and [19] ACCESS____________________ to research institutes, and with voice recognition and synthesis systems able to [20] MIME ____________________ the qualities of personalized human speech, one might [21] JUSTIFY____________________ wonder whether our own electronic replacements are out there on the horizon in the not-too-distant future.

I [22] FUTURE____________________ such as Vernor Vinge and Ray Kurzweil have predicted the eventual emergence of super-intelligences in the form of a "singularity," which would not only encompass all that the human species has ever dreamed, thought, or created, but would also learn and self-replicate with exponential self-improvement, an electronic version of a type of omniscience normally associated with deities.

J But are such projected visions of our future really on the horizon, or is this merely the wishful thinking of adolescent dreamers overcome with exuberance for technology? The human imagination tends to attribute super-human—or more precisely in this scenario, super-super-computer—abilities to our most prized gadgets, often without warrant. As Günther Anders reported in his seminal study of the pathogenesis of the nuclear / computer age, the U.S. Pentagon had seriously considered allowing its—at the time, quite primitive—computers to decide whether or not to use nuclear bombs to combat North Korean and Chinese troops during the Korean War. To anyone with a conscience, the answer should immediately have been patently clear: No! But the excitement that accompanied the [23] NOVEL____________________ of these primitive electronic "brains" allowed many to lose touch with more fundamental questions of the greater good and with what is morally correct and justifiable.

K Today, research in [24] MOLECULE____________________ biology / genetics has opened up other and perhaps even more frightening possibilities than those envisioned in a matrix of artificial intelligences. One must fear that highly acclaimed British writer Kazuo Ishiguro has accurately augured where our technology will one day lead us. In his heart-rending novel, *Never Let Me Go*, Ishiguro portrays the lives and untimely deaths of young human clones whose "sole purpose" in their brief and bitter existence is to serve as living, breathing sources of fresh organs for their wealthy originals: today an eye, tomorrow a kidney, five years from now the brain or the heart. Mission complete.

L Our species' proven track record of base [25] CALLOUS ____________________ and ruthless exploitation of nature and of all the living beings that inhabit her suffices fully to argue that the horror scenario Ishiguro has left to literary posterity is not only possible, but also probable.

POST-READING QUESTIONS

1. In what ways is this final reading passage different from the texts presented in Units 1–11?
2. In your view, why were references not cited in the text?
3. How would you describe the overall tone of the text?
4. Should the author have used a different argument or rhetorical style to make his point?
5. What is the rule for the formation of comparative and superlative adjectives in English?
6. In your own words, describe machine learning.
7. Explain the author's use of the term "instrumental reason" (paragraph B).
8. Explain why the author mentions Kazuo Ishiguro's book *Never Let Me Go*.

VOCABULARY WORK

PART A

From the given text, find the words or phrases that have similar meanings to the words / phrases given in the numbered lists below. The first one is done for you as an example.

From Paragraphs A–F:	Synonymous Word or Phrase
1. sure signs; telltale signs or traits	hallmarks (paragraph B)
2. of a hereditary lineage	____________
3. arcs or paths of flight	____________
4. related to the concept of wholeness and to the idea that the whole is greater than the sum of its parts	____________
5. related to understanding and knowing	____________
6. related to the usefulness of something	____________
7. maintained the same rate of development; maintained the same speed	____________

8. forms or examples serving as models ____________
9. intrusion; infiltration; invasion ____________
10. a wrong name or title ____________
11. to produce in an automated manner ____________
12. replacement; ersatz ____________
13. wonders ____________
14. praised; extolled; hailed; commended ____________
15. svelte; aerodynamic ____________
16. appearing; emerging; coming into view; impending; threatening ____________
17. related to an immediate period of time ____________
18. a point signaling the beginning of a change ____________
19. all-out; untempered; unabated; undiminished ____________
20. chemicals used to kill insects or other pests ____________
21. deadly ____________
22. destroying; reducing to nothingness ____________
23. causing cancer ____________
24. area; forum; scene or place of an event, contest, or battle ____________

From Paragraphs G–L: Synonymous Word or Phrase

25. the will; the act of willing ____________
26. decoded; solved; unscrambled; figured out ____________
27. dazzlingly brilliant; glowing; shining ____________
28. ingenious; extraordinary; special; unprecedented ____________
29. justification; grounds; reason; basis ____________

30. infinite knowledge ____________________

31. occurring too soon or too early ____________________

32. merciless; remorseless; compassionless ____________________

33. future generations ____________________

PART B

VOCABULARY WORK

Choose an appropriate form of one of the words given below to complete the numbered sentences that follow. Two of the words have been used twice.

ARENA	MISNOMER
CARCINOGEN	MITIGATE
COGITATE	PARADIGM
HOLISM	SHORT-TERM
KEEP PACE WITH	STELLAR
LETHAL	SURROGATE
MARVEL	RAVEL

1. Grilled meats contain several dangerous ____________________ that have been linked to stomach cancer and colon cancer.

2. Physicist David Bohm argued that mind and matter are integral aspects of a higher-order ____________________ universe whose essence is information.

3. Many neuroscientists argue that human ____________________ can be completely explained by a reduction of all thought processes to patterns of electrical activity in the brain.

4. Seating 150,000 spectators, Rungnado Stadium in Pyongyang, North Korea, is the largest sporting ____________________ in the world.

5. The human capacity for mercy and compassion has not __________ the development of our instrumental reasoning.

6. Cheating on exams produces at best ____________________ gains at the expense of honest diligence and genuine understanding of the material being tested.

ARENA	MISNOMER
CARCINOGEN	MITIGATE
COGITATE	PARADIGM
HOLISM	SHORT-TERM
KEEP PACE WITH	STELLAR
LETHAL	SURROGATE
MARVEL	RAVEL

7. Until the dawn of general relativity and quantum mechanics in the early twentieth century, classical Newtonian physics had reigned supreme as the unquestioned ______________________ of scientific inquiry.

8. The bite of the Common Krait (genus Bungarus), commonly found in southern Asia, is quite ______________________, with a mortality rate of about 50% even for victims who receive antivenom.

9. The as yet only partially understood ability of cephalopods, such as the octopus and the cuttlefish, to camouflage themselves perfectly and almost instantaneously into the background patterns of their immediate environment is a truly astounding ______________________ of nature.

10. Married couples who for whatever reason are unable to conceive or bear children themselves often hire the services of a ______________________ mother, who for pay becomes impregnated through in vitro fertilization.

11. Violinist Anne-Akiko Meyer's ______________________ performance of the notoriously difficult Sibelius violin concerto was the true highpoint of the musical season.

12. ______________________ the mysterious origin of the Big Bang would likely be the greatest theoretical accomplishment in human history; the question is, however, whether the question itself is even answerable.

13. ______________________ acts of cruelty and aggression are often telltale signs of severely impaired or undeveloped regions in the brains of individuals predisposed to sociopathic behavior.

14. The name "English horn" for the tenor member of the oboe family is a true ______________________ because the double-reed woodwind is not English in origin, nor is it a horn.

15. Shy individuals often ________________________ at the ability of intrepid extroverts to strike up a conversation with virtually anyone, at any time, under any circumstances.

16. The ingestion of mercury primarily through the consumption of contaminated seafood often leads to significant ______________________ impairment and to kidney damage.

PART C

LANGUAGE FOCUS

1. Who is likely the intended audience of this text?

2. What type (genre) of text is this? What message is the author intending to send?

3. What two types of thought are being contrasted in this text?

4. In paragraph D, what does the possessive pronoun "their" refer to in the third sentence?

5. What word could best replace "warrant" in the phrase "super-super-computer abilities to our most prized gadgets, often without warrant" in paragraph J?

Sentence Transformation

For questions 6–10, use the word given below the first sentence to complete the second sentence in the blanks provided. Use between three and eight words including the given word. The given word must NOT be changed in any way, and the meaning of the sentences should be as similar as possible.

Example: We eagerly await a renewed encounter with you in the future.
forward
We are really <u>looking forward to seeing</u> you again in the future.

6. Unfortunately, we had to close last year because too few people were using our services.
demand
Unfortunately, we had to close last year because there ______________
____ our services.

7. We found the clerk's aggressive sales pitch very disconcerting and annoying.

   aback

   We were quite ______________________________

   the clerk's aggressive sales pitch.

8. We'd advise you to take full advantage of the low interest rates and shop around for better mortgage terms.

   avail

   We'd advise you ______________________________

   the low interest rates and shop around for better mortgage terms.

9. Would you like to contribute something for the birthday gift we're buying the director?

   chip

   Would you like ______________________________

   for the gift we're buying the director for her birthday?

10. The Great Pyramids of Egypt have endured for millennia.

    test

    The Great Pyramids of Egypt have ______________________

    time.

ULTIMATE CHALLENGE

PART D

Sentence Reconstruction

Reconstruct the following ten sentences by putting the individual words back into their correct order. All of the sentences represent TRUE statements that can be inferred from the information presented in the reading text. Supply appropriate punctuation as needed.

1. the the for on has cognitive conditions human earth apparatus permanently planet life altered

   ____

   ____

   ____

2. of of the the in with numbers has resulted untold human species environment interaction extinction

3. of of of of a the the all is thought total perfection life capable perversion terrestrial weapons annihilation

4. over on for of a a the as has instrumental all sustainable life environment heavy nature habitat toll utilitarian reason's forms conquest taken

5. term term the of are our than better humans comprehending activities solutions long short for at at problems much devising effects synergistic

6. a a the to with from is whole consumer our qualities human items abstract given largely preoccupation result specific tendency of

7. the a of into and involves system's learning computer integration feedback constant positive database machine negative

8. by on databases skilled computers like developed enormous IBM's programmers elaborate rely highly probability and "WATSON" algorithms

____

____

____

9. the to that one futurologists self-replicate become have ability will self-aware predicted day some computers with

____

____

____

10. to a the with for back our has empathy gadgetry capacity fads taken seat human and preoccupation

____

____

____

LANGUAGE IN USE

PART E

I Suggested Questions for Discussion

A. On a scale of 1–10, with 10 being an extreme optimist and 1 being an extreme pessimist, describe yourself and give reasons for your own optimism or pessimism.

B. Philosophers are by definition "big picture" thinkers; accountants, carpenters, and dentists, in contrast, tend to be very detailed, thing- or procedure-oriented people who live in the concrete "here and now." On a scale of 1–10, with 10 being a thoroughly "big picture" person and 1 being a "no-nonsense" / "nothing-but-the-facts-I-can-see" type, describe yourself and give reasons for your own self-assessment.

C. Based on your own observations and life experience, explain why you agree or disagree with the views presented by the author of the essay in this unit.

II Suggested Questions for Written Research Projects

A. Write a reflective essay in which you argue for or against the positions presented in the essay at the beginning of this unit.

B. If you could make the world to your own liking, what changes would you make and why?

C. Describe and outline your own topic-related research question.

APPENDIX

A

REGISTER IN ENGLISH

Register referes to the difference between formal and informal English. For the working professional, a shift in register in the wrong direction can spell disaster. Imagine that you feel severe chest pain. Fearing you might have a serious heart condition, you muster up enough courage to see a competent specialist who greets you in his office with the comment, "Dude, that is like so not cool to be so wiped out like that. Bummer!" Very few of us would entertain even for a second the thought of having this man open up our chest to perform bypass surgery!

At the other end of the spectrum, an office colleague with whom we share close quarters and on whose cooperation we depend daily might come across as cold, distant, or even silly if the language s/he uses is overly formal: "I hereby reimburse you for the total cost of the pen which I inadvertently damaged while performing a writing assignment yesterday."

Of course there are many degrees of formality, and most written English (including newspapers, magazines, and novels) is situated somewhere between the two extremes. Most business letters are also written in the "middle" to "upper" registers, whereas correspondence in the legal professions and in diplomatic circles tends to favor the upper register. Emails today are often written in the lower to middle register. The "lower" register includes most terms that express intimacy, endearment, or affection; common slang; and vulgar expressions (e.g., "bullshit"). As a general, but non-binding rule, words and expressions derived from French and Latin tend to be of upper register, whereas those of German (for example, most all phrasal verbs) or of old Anglo-Saxon origin tend to be put in the middle to lower registers.

Listed below are a few examples of words from the middle and upper registers:

Middle Register	Upper Register
think	deem; regard
think about	contemplate; consider
liar	prevaricator
work	labor; function
get	obtain
stop	cease
begin	commence; initiate
keep	retain
hope	aspire
look into	investigate; examine
so	therefore; thus
cook; make	prepare
figure out	solve; determine; calculate
hateful	odious
cute	attractive; appealing
then; later	subsequently
watch	observe

APPENDIX

B

DEPENDENT CLAUSES

There are three general types of dependent clauses in English: **RELATIVE CLAUSES** (also called "adjective clauses"), **ADVERB CLAUSES**, and **NOUN CLAUSES.**

I. RELATIVE CLAUSES

Just like adjectives, relative (or adjective) clauses modify nouns. They help to connect two ideas or thought groups together. In their non-reduced form, adjective clauses begin with a **CLAUSE MARKER** such as WHO, THAT, WHICH, WHOSE, or the relative adverbs WHEN and WHERE. If the clause marker is the object of the verb or a preposition in the relative clause, we can often omit the marker. And, if the verb phrase in the relative clause is a passive, we can often omit the marker as well as the auxiliary verb.

The book [that] *I bought last week is really interesting.*
[that] is the object of "bought."

Magnetic resonance imaging (MRI) is one of the most important diagnostic tools [that are] used in medical technology.
[that are used] is a passive verb phrase.

WHO is used exclusively for people, NOT for things or even for pets.

e.g.: The woman **who** won the race is from Kenya.

WHOSE is used for relationships that entail some type of possession.

e.g.: The man **whose** wife is president of the company has just been awarded a $2 million bonus.

WHOM is very formal and is used only in formal contexts. In this case, it marks an object case (Latin: *casus accusativus*).

e.g.: The woman **whom** Parliament chose to lead the panel received her Ph.D. from the University of Cambridge.

In this sentence, "Parliament" is the subject of the relative (= adjective) clause and **whom** functions as the object of the verb "chose."

Non-Defining (=Non-Identifying) versus Defining (=Identifying) Clauses

Compare these sentences:

A) John's wife, **who is a dentist**, plays golf and tennis.
= NON-DEFINING / NON-IDENTIFYING CLAUSE

B) Ted's wife **who is a dentist** has her own airplane.
= DEFINING / IDENTIFYING CLAUSE

Sentence A is a neutral sentence because it tells us that John is married to a female dentist and that she likes to play golf and tennis. The relative clause is said to be non-defining because it only adds extra information about John's wife; the relative clause does not serve to distinguish John's wife from his other wives because he has only one wife.

Sentence B, however, is not a neutral sentence because we are informed that Ted is married to at least TWO women, one of whom is a dentist and owns her own airplane. The relative clause **defines / identifies** WHICH of Ted's wives we are talking about.

Compare this pair of example sentences:

A) I took my car to the repair shop, **which has a two-day service.**
NON-DEFINING / NON-IDENTIFYING CLAUSE

B) I took my car to the repair shop **that has 24-hour service.**
DEFINING / IDENTIFYING CLAUSE

From A) we can conclude that there is only one repair shop in the town. From B) we conclude that there are two or perhaps many more, and that one of them has a 24-hour service.

Notice that in the second of the pairs of sentences (i.e., the defining clause), "which" can be replaced with the word "**that**." "Which" cannot be replaced with "that" in sentence A.

Defining Relative Clauses

- **NO commas** are used to separate the relative clause.
- We can replace "who" or "which" with "that."
- If the relative pronoun in the relative clause is the object of a verb or a preposition, it can be omitted, as in this sentence:

  The film I saw was excellent.

  The **non-reduced** form of the clause would be:

  The film that I saw was excellent.

  "that" functions as the object of the verb "saw" and can thus be omitted.

Further:

The doctor we spoke to is a specialist in sports injuries.

The most formal unreduced form of the clause here would read:

The doctor to whom we spoke is a specialist in sports injuries.

"whom" is the object of the preposition "to" and can thus be omitted, and the preposition "to" is placed after the verb.

Non-Defining Relative Clauses

- **Commas** are needed to separate non-defining clauses from the dependent clause.
- The relative clause markers "who," "which," or "whom" CANNOT be replaced by "that."
- The relative pronoun cannot be omitted.

Example: *Phillip's brother, who has just become mayor of his city, has four sons.*

SPECIAL NOTE: The relative clause marker can often be eliminated, thus reducing the relative clause, if any of the following special conditions are met:

A. subject + to be + adjective / subject + to be + prepositional phrase

Hong Kong, which is situated on numerous islands in the South China Sea, has become the most important financial center in Asia.

The independent clause is a complete sentence in its own right:

Hong Kong has become the most important financial center in Asia.

The non-defining relative clause adds additional information and conforms to the structure given above. We can thus reduce the clause to read:

Hong Kong, situated on numerous islands in the South China Sea, has become the most important financial center in Asia.

Second example:

The castle, which is too far gone to be repaired, will have to be torn down.

This sentence can be reduced to:

The castle, too far gone to be repaired, will have to be torn down.

B. Passive Voice

The picture, which was published in the New Economic Times, *shows the governor accepting a bribe.*

Because the relative clause is written in the passive voice, the clause can be reduced to read:

The picture, published in the New Economic Times, *shows the governor accepting a bribe.*

Second example:

The house, which was constructed in 1852, is believed to be haunted.

This sentence can be reduced to:

The house, constructed in 1852, is believed to be haunted.
[The reduced clause eliminates the relative pronoun and the auxiliary verb, but retains the past participle of the lexical verb.]

Completed in 80 AD under Emperor Titus, the Colosseum is the most iconic representation of Imperial Roman architecture.

[In this example, the reduced relative clause has been placed as the first element in the sentence, pre-positional to the sentence subject. In its unreduced form, the sentence would read: "The Colosseum, which was completed in 80 AD under Emperor Titus, is the most iconic representation of Imperial Roman architecture."]

C. subject + to be + noun

Firuza, who is a student from Saudi Arabia, is majoring in econometrics.

This sentence can be reduced to:

Firuza, a student from Saudi Arabia, is majoring in econometrics.

D. Verbs That Imply Inherent or Permanent Characteristics

The 390-meter mountain that overlooks the Guanabara Bay in Rio de Janeiro is known as "Sugarloaf."

This sentence can be reduced to:

The 390-meter mountain overlooking the Guanabara Bay in Rio de Janeiro is known as "Sugarloaf." [Note that the original finite verb in the relative clause ("overlooks") is changed to the present participle in the reduced clause.]

E. Verbs That Imply a Continuous Activity

The woman who is designing the concert hall is originally from Iraq.

This sentence can be reduced to:

The woman designing the concert hall is originally from Iraq. [The reduced clause eliminates the relative pronoun and the auxiliary verb.]

II. ADVERB CLAUSES

Like adverbs, **ADVERB CLAUSES** provide information about the circumstances or conditions in which an activity takes place. Structurally, adverb clauses consist of a CLAUSE MARKER plus a clause subject and a clause verb. The main types of adverb clauses are:

- cause and effect
- condition
- contrast
- time
- purpose
- opposition
- negative condition

Examples of each type:

Cause / Effect

Because Susan had already seen the movie, she didn't go with her friends to see it again.

["Because" is the adverb clause marker; "Susan" is the adverb clause subject; "had already seen" is the adverb clause verb; "the movie" is the object of the adverb clause verb; "she didn't go with her friends to see it again" is the independent clause.]

Frequent clause markers include: *as, because, since, for.*

Condition

If my mother were here, she would bake us an apple pie.

[This is a SECOND CONDITION CLAUSE. "If" is the adverb clause marker; "my mother" is the adverb clause subject; "were" is the subjunctive mood of "be" required for the second conditional; "here" is an adverbial; "she would bake us an apple pie" is the independent clause.]

Frequent clause markers include: *as long as, if, on condition that, when.*

Contrast or Opposition

While most Asians tend to eat rice with their meals, Italians often prefer pasta.

["While" is the adverb clause marker of contrast; "most Asians" is the adverb clause subject; "tend to eat" is the verb phrase; "rice with their meals" is the object phrase; "Italians often prefer pasta" is the independent clause.]

Even though Carla is fond of driving, she refuses to buy a car.

["Even though" is the adverb clause marker of opposition; "Carla" is the adverb clause subject; "is" is the adverb clause verb; "fond of driving" is a complement phrase; "she refuses to buy a car" is the independent clause.]

Frequent clause markers include: *although, even though, nevertheless, though, while.*

Manner, Place and Time

Manner

Samantha is grinning as if she doesn't have a care in the world.

["Samantha is grinning" is the independent clause; "as if" is the adverb clause marker of manner; "she" is the adverb clause subject; "doesn't have" is the adverb clause verb phrase; "a care in the world" is the object phrase of the verb "doesn't have."]

Frequent clause markers of MANNER include: *as, as if, as though.*

Place

You may take a seat wherever you can find a chair.

["You may take a seat" is the independent clause; "wherever" is the adverb clause marker of place; "you" is the adverb clause subject; "can find" is the adverb clause verb phrase; "a chair" is the object of the adverb clause verb phrase.]

Frequent clause markers include: *where, wherever.*

Time

When I woke up this morning, I heard the birds singing outside my bedroom window.

["When" is the adverb clause marker; "I" is the adverb clause subject; "woke up" is the adverb clause verb; "this morning" is an adverbial phrase; "I heard the birds singing outside my bedroom window" is the independent clause.]

Frequent clause markers include: *after, as, as soon as, before, by the time, once, since, until / till, when, whenever.*

Purpose

Martin is going to St. Petersburg for three months so that he can improve his speaking skills in Russian.

["Martin is going to St. Petersburg for three months" is the independent clause; "so that" is the adverb clause marker of purpose; "he" is the adverb clause subject; "can improve" is the adverb clause verb; "his speaking skills in Russian" is the adverb clause object phrase.]

Frequent clause markers include: *in order to, so, so that.*

Negative Condition

Unless our region receives substantial rain this month, we'll have to ration water.

["Unless" is the adverb clause marker of negative condition; "our region" is the adverb clause subject; "receives" is the adverb clause verb; "substantial rain this month" is the object phrase; "we'll have to ration water" is the independent clause.]

Frequent clause markers include: *unless*

Reduced Adverb Clauses

If the subject of the adverb clause and the subject of the independent clause are identical, then the adverb clause can often be reduced by eliminating the adverb clause subject and any auxiliary verbs and changing the finite verb to either a present or a past participle. The adverb clause marker itself must be kept. [NOTE: **NEVER REDUCE** adverb clauses after "because" or "by the time."]

Using sentences from pages 218 and 219 as examples:

Having already seen the movie, Susan didn't go with her friends to see it again.

When waking up this morning, I heard the birds singing outside my bedroom window.

[This sentence could also be reduced further to read: *Waking up this morning, I heard the birds ...*]

Even though fond of driving, Carla refuses to buy a car.

III. NOUN CLAUSES

Just like nouns themselves, **NOUN CLAUSES** function as either *subjects, objects*, or *complements.*

Structurally, noun clauses generally consist of a NOUN CLAUSE MARKER, a NOUN CLAUSE SUBJECT, a NOUN CLAUSE VERB, and optionally an object, complement, or adverbial. Noun clause markers include:

- all *wh-question* words / phrases such as *who? what? when? where? why? how? how much? how many? how often?*
- *that*
- *whether*
- *if*

Examples:

a) Noun clause subject:

What we want to know is the name of the company.

b) Noun clause complement:

The question is why he quit his job.

c) Noun clause object:

We would like to know why he quit his last position.
Karen wanted to know if I liked spaghetti.

When used as a noun clause marker, "that" can often be omitted if the noun clause itself is used as the object of the main verb in the sentence:

e.g. *She said that they were going to Hawaii on vacation.*

"that they were going to Hawaii on vacation" is the OBJECT of the verb "said," so the word "that" can be (and in spoken discourse most often is) eliminated:

She said they were going to Hawaii on vacation.

APPENDIX C

GERUNDS AND INFINITIVES

Both gerunds and infinitives are used as nouns in sentences, meaning that they can take on the functions of subjects, objects, or complements. **Gerunds** are lexical verbs + the *-ing* ending, making them look essentially like present participles, but unlike present participles, gerunds function grammatically as nouns in sentences, while still retaining the "flavor" of the verbs they are derived from. **Full infinitives** consist of "to" plus the base form of the lexical verb.

Examples: *Diving in submarine caves can be quite dangerous.*
[Gerund sentence subject]

To err is human.
[Full infinitive sentence subject]

I like walking in the autumn leaves.
[Gerund object of the verb "like"]

My wife likes to swim.
[Full infinitive object of the verb "likes"]

His goal is running the mile in record time.
[Gerund complement of the verb "is"]

Her goal is to be the best oboist in her region.
[Full infinitive complement of the verb "is"]

English recognizes a number of fixed idiomatic combinations that **require** either the full infinitive or the gerund after certain verbs. With a number of such verbs, the meaning remains essentially unchanged regardless of whether a gerund or an infinitive is used.

Example: *I like to bake cookies. / I like baking cookies.*

There are exceptions, however. For example:

He stopped eating.

The use of the gerund after "stop" means that the action denoted by the gerund has ceased completely. This contrasts sharply with: *He stopped to eat.* In this latter sentence, the man stopped whatever he was previously doing *in order to eat.*

Similarly, the meaning in these two sentences shifts as well:

She remembered to lock the doors of the house. / She remembered locking the doors of the house.

In the first sentence, the implication is that the woman was under some type of obligation to lock the doors of the house and she fulfilled that obligation. In the second sentence, the focus of the sentence shifts onto the woman's memory. Perhaps she received a concussion and could no longer remember anything except for the fact that she locked the doors of the house.

The following list contains many of the most commonly used idiomatic collocations of verbs in conjunction with gerunds and infinitives.

Verbs Followed by Gerunds

admit	dislike	practice	risk
advise	enjoy	prefer	can't stand
anticipate	finish	quit	start
appreciate	forget	recall	stop
avoid	hate	recollect	suggest
can't bear	can't help	recommend	tolerate
begin	keep	regret	try
complete	like	remember	understand [often with a personal noun or pronoun]
consider	love	resent [usually with a personal noun or pronoun]	
continue	mention	resist	
delay	mind		
deny	miss		
discuss	postpone		

Verbs Followed by Infinitives

afford
agree
appear
arrange
ask
aspire
can't bear
beg
begin
care
claim
consent
continue
decide
demand
deserve
expect
fail
forget
hate
hesitate
hope
learn
like
love
manage
mean
need
offer
plan
prefer
prepare
pretend
promise
refuse
regret
remember
seem
can't stand
start
struggle
swear
threaten
try
volunteer
wait
want
wish

Verbs Followed by Pronoun + Infinitive

advise
allow
ask
beg
cause
challenge
convince
dare
encourage
expect
forbid
force
hire
inspire
instruct
invite
need
order
permit
persuade
remind
require
teach
tell
urge
want
warn

APPENDIX

D

COLLOCATION OF VERBS AND PREPOSITIONS

(with example sentences)

VERBS + *about*

argue

My parents were arguing about two political candidates all during dinner last night.

be concerned

The teachers don't appear to be at all concerned about the low test scores.

be worried

I'm very worried about my uncle's heart condition; he's headed for surgery yet again.

boast

Greg was boasting again about how much money he made last month.

brag

I can't endure people who brag about how much they own and make.

care

Susan seems to care too much about the opinions of other people.

cry

There's no use crying about the money you lost in Vegas; it's gone now.

dream

Last night, I dreamed about the music teacher I had in elementary school.

fret

Ted frets about his health so much that he's going to make himself sick.

protest

Students were protesting about the massive increases in tuition fees.

rant

My choleric boss was ranting about the excessive consumption of coffee at work.

scream

My neighbor was screaming about the cars that were illegally parked in front of her house.

talk

Joan and her husband must have been talking about something private when I walked into the room because they stopped immediately when they saw me.

worry

Mickie is very worried about her son's low test scores in algebra.

VERBS + *against*

argue

Most financial advisors would argue against taking out a second mortgage on your home.

count

Coming to work late two weeks in a row is going to count against you in terms of merit pay.

insure

In California, homeowners must insure their property against earthquake damage.

protest

Trade unions are protesting against the government's new wage laws.

VERBS + *at*

glance

I quickly glanced at my phone to see what time it was before leaving for work.

glare

The boss just glared at me when I criticized her decision to hire more people.

guess

The room was literally packed, so we could only guess at how many people were there.

hint

My boyfriend was hinting at how much weight he thought I'd gained.

look

My roommate was looking at his bank statements when I walked into his room.

marvel

The entire audience marveled at the violinist's virtuosity.

succeed

Some people seem to succeed at business quite naturally without even really trying.

VERBS + *for*

account

The current laws of physics can't account for the inflationary expansion of the universe.

allow

Current tax laws will not allow for any further deductions this quarter.

apologize

I sincerely apologize for forgetting our dinner date.

bargain

The Schultz's new house construction project has turned out to be far more work than they had bargained for.

blame

Our department is being blamed for the company's significant loss in revenue this year.

care

Many people simply do not care for coriander, which is also known as "cilantro."

charge

The airlines charged us $400 for excess luggage weight.

count

How much will my volunteer service with the Peace Corps count for on my resume?

earmark

The county government has earmarked this land for a nature preserve.

pay

The dinner we had at the restaurant was so expensive we couldn't pay for it in cash, so we used our credit card.

sell

One landscape image made by an up-and-coming photographer sold for $1.5 million.

VERBS + *from*

bar

After the witness's violent outburst, she was barred from the courtroom.

benefit

Everyone benefits significantly from moderate daily exercise.

differ

Today, industrial computer designs do not differ significantly from one another.

distinguish

It's often difficult to distinguish natural from synthetic gemstones.

distract

How many young people are routinely distracted from their studies by the urge to engage in social media exchanges?

exempt

Most governments exempt people with severe physical disabilities from military service.

expel

The two men were expelled from the country on charges of industrial espionage.

refrain

The management kindly asks the audience to refrain from talking or using their phones during the performance.

resign

The prime minister was asked to resign from office after bribery charges were brought against him.

result

Obesity usually results from an excess intake of calories and sugar.

stem

The food shortages today stem from the severe drought we experienced last summer.

suffer

Many elderly people suffer from painful osteoarthritis.

VERBS + *in*

be

My friend was not in when I stopped by her house.

be absorbed

Rachel didn't even hear the phone ring because she was so absorbed in the novel she was reading.

be engrossed

The two women were so engrossed in their conversation that they didn't realize the store had closed.

confide

Dana knew she could always confide in her best friend.

involve

My neighbor got a black eye when he became involved in an altercation between a man and his wife.

major

My brother is majoring in law at university.

result

The ongoing construction work in our part of town has resulted in significant traffic jams.

specialize

My cousin first studied general medicine, but then went on to specialize in endocrinology.

succeed

So far, scientists have not succeeded in developing an effective vaccine against HIV.

VERBS + *of*

accuse

Our boss is being accused of embezzling funds from the company accounts.

convict

Julius and Ethel Rosenberg were convicted of espionage and executed in the United States.

cure

Working in the chocolate factory for six months has cured me of my chocolate addiction.

die

Margaret died of natural causes at the age of 101.

suspect

Terry had initially been suspected of killing his wife, until she unexpectedly turned up one day months later.

VERBS + on

base

The prosecution will base its case on DNA evidence and eyewitness testimony.

be based

This murder conviction was based largely on circumstantial evidence.

blame

Someone put ink on the teacher's seat and everyone blamed it on me.

center

Our new advertising strategy centers on a clear shift in demographics.

concentrate

I find it very difficult to concentrate on anything academic if there's a lot of noise in the room.

congratulate

We need to send Yongzhi and Jianqi a card to congratulate them on the birth of their daughter.

decide

You'll soon need to decide on what type of food you want for the company party.

elaborate

Would you care to elaborate on the details of your new novel?

impose

The new coalition has imposed strict guidelines on the use of any form of pesticides in farming.

insist

My professor insists on being called by his full title: Professor Dr. Schmidt.

sit

The government sat on the unflattering data and prayed that it wouldn't come to light.

work

We're going to work on improving our sales this quarter with a new advertising campaign.

VERBS + *to*

amount

Your children will never amount to anything if they don't learn the importance of self-discipline.

answer

Who does your boss answer to?

appeal

The combination of brown and purple doesn't really appeal to me.

apply

These guidelines do not apply to part-time employees.

attribute

Our head office attributes the downturn in sales to the particularly harsh winter.

be used

I'm simply not used to being the only conservative voter in the family.

cater

Our new clothing line caters to a wide variety of tastes and age groups.

commit

David has committed himself to writing one novel per year.

confess

The young boy finally confessed to putting gum in the girl's hair.

contribute

All that Gena contributed to the last office party was a single bottle of wine.

devote

James has devoted himself to improving the health and welfare of animals around the world.

prefer

Astonishing numbers of people actually prefer to give than to receive.

react

The professor simply didn't react to the student's remark about sexy underwear.

refer

I think my niece was referring to the boy she recently met when her eyes lit up.

resort

Since these asocial neighbors have not responded to our appeals, we'll have to resort to legal action against them.

see

Could you see to the garden and our mail while we're on vacation?

subject

Synthetic diamonds are produced by subjecting carbon to extreme heat and pressure.

talk

Almost all people need someone to talk to when they're depressed.

VERBS + *with*

acquaint

I'd like to acquaint you with my dear friend, Chloe, who also shares your avid interest in computer games.

argue

Sue has been arguing with her husband a lot lately about their troublesome son.

associate

I personally associate intelligence with a passion for reading.

be concerned

I refuse to be concerned with trivial matters like hairstyles and wardrobe.

be faced

Our government is faced with an unprecedented budget deficit that most likely cannot ever be repaid.

charge

George is being charged with reckless endangerment.

clash

The Left clashes with the Right when it comes to the unions' demands.

coincide

This month, the solar eclipse coincides with the celestial alignment of five planets.

collide

I collided with a garbage truck as I was backing out of my driveway this morning.

comply

The company is refusing to comply with the government's new export restrictions.

confront

If we don't do our best to save money, we'll be confronted with an uncontrollable amount of debt.

confuse

We often confuse the oboe with the clarinet, even though they are very different instruments.

deal

One of the most difficult challenges for teachers is having to deal with unruly children.

fill

Please fill all the empty bottles with tap water.

meet

We're meeting with representatives of our Japanese subsidiary to discuss our plans to expand in the Asian markets.

plead

The accused man pleaded with the judge to show mercy.

provide

Regrettably, you won't be provided with any form of paid transportation to and from the hotel.

talk

We'll need to talk with the girl's parents to see if they can reason with her.

tamper

Immediately throw away any purchased food or medicinal item that appears to have been tampered with.

work

We're working with a number of governmental and military agencies to ensure the safety and welfare of Africa's elephants.

APPENDIX E

INVERSION

We often INVERT the normal word order in English to achieve a more dramatic or emphatic effect. Compare the following sentences:

a) I don't ever want to hear you say that again.
b) Never do I want to hear you say that again.

In the eyes and ears of all native speakers of English, sentence b is clearly much more emphatic and dramatic; in fact, the sentence sounds quite aggressive and determined. Inversion is achieved by placing a negative adverbial phrase at the beginning of the sentence and then simply adding a question form in the appropriate tense. In the above example, "Never" is the negative adverbial, which is then followed by what looks to be a question form in the simple present: "do I want to hear you say that again."

Negative adverbials include the following words and phrases:

- at no time
- at no point
- never
- not once
- not until
- on no account
- on no condition
- rarely
- seldom
- under no condition
- under no circumstances

Examples:

1) At no time during the meal *did they mention having problems with money.*
2) Not once *did they make eye contact during the party.*
3) Under no circumstances *is the director to be disturbed.*
4) Never *have I seen such an infuriating woman.*
5) Seldom *have we met with a more obstinate client.*
6) Not until he quits his job *will he realize how important a regular income is.*

With *be*-verbs involving subjects and sentence complements, the subject normally switches positions in the sentence with the complement for emphatic inversion. At the same time, good writers must strive to maintain a subjective sense of balance in terms of the overall stylistic "appeal" of the sentence.

Examples:

1. *The country's high debt levels are of major concern.*

[Sentence subject = "the country's high debt levels"; complement = "of major concern"]

The more emphatic inversion would read:

Of major concern are the country's high debt levels.

2. The committee's refusal even to consider our proposals has been especially aggravating.

[Sentence subject = "the committee's refusal even to consider our proposals"; complement = "especially aggravating"]

The emphatic inversion would read:

Especially aggravating has been the committee's refusal even to consider our proposals.

APPENDIX

F

PASSIVES

In order to hide or de-emphasize the agent or author of an action, or in order to shift the focus from the "doer" onto the process or subject matter at hand, we often use the PASSIVE VOICE.

Example: (At the hotel reception):

You are not allowed to smoke here.

In a number of cultures, this sentence might come across as unduly aggressive and direct, and hence highly inappropriate. To remove the "sting" from the sentence, we could simply place the sentence into the equivalent passive form:

Smoking isn't allowed here.

Grammatically, the passive is obtained quite simply, as exemplified in the following transformation.

ACTIVE: *The wasp stung the boy.*
PASSIVE: *The boy was stung by a wasp.*

"The wasp" is the subject of the passive sentence; "stung" is the simple past tense of the lexical verb "sting"; "the boy" is the object of the verb.

The OBJECT of the active sentence becomes the subject of the passive sentence: "The boy"

The passive verb phrase consists of the appropriate tense of the verb *be* (in this case "was" as the simple past form corresponding to the 3rd person singular subject) plus the past participle of the lexical verb: *stung.*

The SUBJECT of the active sentence becomes the "agent" of the passive sentence BUT only if it is necessary to indicate who or what the agent is.

Example:

ACTIVE: *A thief stole an original Van Gogh painting from the museum.*
PASSIVE: *An original Van Gogh painting was stolen from the museum.*

(Since the verb "steal" essentially connotes the illegal taking of something by a thief, and since "the thief" in question is unknown, we should omit the agent.)

Example:

ACTIVE: *They are reconstructing significant sections of Rome's Coliseum.*
PASSIVE: *Significant sections of Rome's Coliseum are being reconstructed.*

APPENDIX G

CONDITIONALS

CONDITIONALS represent a special category of adverb clauses. Because of both their importance for all forms of discourse and their frequency of use, conditionals also normally form a separate focal point in the learning process.

English recognizes FOUR distinct conditionals: the ZERO, the FIRST, the SECOND, and the THIRD. Given below is the skeletal form and purpose of each.

ZERO Conditional

When + subject + simple present, subject + simple present.

The Zero Conditional describes processes and procedures, many of which express a "when → then" relationship.

Time frame: TIMELESS

Example Sentences:

"When you press [verb in the present simple] the green button, the machine switches [present simple] on."

"When tectonic plates deep beneath the earth's surface shift [verb in the present simple], earthquakes occur [present simple]."

FIRST Conditional

If + subject + simple present, subject + [future with "will"] or [imperative].

The First Conditional states real possibilities that may or may not happen.

Time frame: PRESENT or FUTURE [with a few exceptions]

Example Sentence:

"If stocks continue [simple present] to fall, the company will have to seek [future with 'will'] investment from other sources."

SECOND Conditional

If + subject + verb form of the simple past, subject + modal + infinitive without "to."

The Second Conditional is used in speculation or hypothetical reasoning about the present or future. NOTE: If the verb in the If-clause is "be," the "be"-verb changes to "were" for all grammatical subjects. [Slang and spoken English frequently permit the use of "was" for the 3rd person singular.]

Time frame: PRESENT or FUTURE

Example Sentence:

"If corporate CEOs were ["be"-verb changes to "were"] ethically more responsible, investors might have [modal + infinitive without "to"] more confidence to invest in the market."

THIRD Conditional

If + subject + past perfect, subject + modal + infinitive without "to."

The Third Conditional is used in speculation or hypothetical reasoning about the past.

Time frame: PAST

Example Sentence:

"If a few brave women hadn't come [past perfect] forward to reveal company secrets, the Enron scandal might never have been disclosed." [modal + present perfect infinitive without "to"]

JJ Polk, PhD, completed his post-doctoral teaching credentials in the UK with an UCLES Diploma. A former CELTA tutor and IELTS examiner, Polk has lived and taught in Europe, the Middle East, and the Far East. He now teaches at the University of Southern California in Los Angeles and is especially interested in interdisciplinary perspectives on pragmatics in communication.

www.ingramcontent.com/pod-product-compliance
Lightning Source LLC
Chambersburg PA
CBHW081220170426
43198CB00017B/2665
* 9 7 8 0 9 9 0 9 0 8 6 2 3 *